STOWM͟ ͟ ͟ ͟ET
-
COMBS

AND
STOWUPLAND
PUBS

Cheers!

Neil L͟

by Neil Langridge & Brian A Southgate

ISBN 978-0-9562243-1-6

Published by Polstead Press
5A The Maltings, Stowupland Road, Stowmarket,
Suffolk IP14 5AG

Tel: 01449 677500
Fax: 01449 770028
Email: info@ghyllhouse.co.uk

Acknowledgements

Many people have contributed information and pictures of the
public houses detailed in this book and of the people associated
with them. We hope we have remembered everyone but apologise
for any omissions.

Adnams Plc, Ashley Barnard, Mary Beasley, Pam Bishop, Jenny Beaumont,
Susan Beaumont-Rudderham, Pauline Biggs, Barbara Bush, Val Chenery, Brian
Cobbold, Ivan Codd, Dudley Diaper, the late Harry Double, Maxine Douglas,
Sheree Ellis, Ralph Griffith, Bob Hall, the late George Harratt, Desmond
Herring, Sheila Hudgell, Richard Pitkin, John Riches, Dennis Reynolds, Alex
Tory, Terry Waller, Lesley Ward, Paul Ward, Steve Williams, Sue Williams, Jill
Wright, the staff of the Suffolk County Record Offices.

Contents

Introduction

"There is nothing which has yet been contrived by man, by which so much happiness is produced as by a good tavern or inn."
Boswell: Life of Samuel Johnson

The origins of the English inn are intimately connected with travel and with the needs of travellers to obtain food and a nights accommodation, the provision of beer would have been taken for granted in a time before a reliable supply of clean drinking water.

Inns

Stowmarket being a thoroughfare town, situated as it is midway between Ipswich to the East and Bury St. Edmunds to the West would be an obvious place to break the journey. There would have been some competition from Inns in Needham Market and other villages on route. The number of such travellers was probably relatively small until the coming of regular coach travel in the18[th] century. Stowmarket's status as the premier market town for the area, meant that on Thursdays inns such as the Kings Head and the White Hart would be at their busiest, thus a whole service industry of innkeepers, chambermaids, ostlers, brewers and cooks would have grown up to supply this need.

Alehouses

The smaller alehouse or beerhouse would have had a different origin. When ale or beer was drunk by everyone from children to farm labourers brewing was as much part of the housewife's routine as baking, thus brewing was seen as a predominantly female activity. The weekly brew was a routine part of a woman's household tasks and it would have been a logical step to brew a larger amount and sell the surplus to supplement the household income. A woman who brewed ale for sale was termed a brewster, if she bought ale from another brewer to sell, the term was a huckster. The beer would either be sold in the street or from the home, often a room being put aside for drinking on the premises, sometimes the alehouse was no more than this.

Definitions

Several terms are used in this book to describe premises licensed to sell beer, wine and spirits. These names originally would have each had a specific meaning, but later became interchangeable. An inn had to provide bed and board for travellers. A Tavern would also be licensed to serve wine. Alehouses or later beerhouses would have been smaller establishments licensed to sell only beer. The Public House really only dates from Victorian times and covers all these establishments.

Beer versus Ale

The terms Beer and Ale have also become interchangeable but strictly speaking beer is flavoured with hops while ale is not. Hopped beer was not introduced into England from northern Europe until the early 15th Century, at first there was a great deal of prejudice against hops and the foreign brewers who had bought them to this country, beer brewers and ale brewers remaining distinct trades. The eventual acceptance of beer over ale was probably due to the preservative qualities that hops imparted to beer, as ale could not be kept long.

The development of Inns and Beerhouses

Before the 18th century most inns were grouped around the marketplace. Gradually shops and inns spread along Ipswich Street, Bury Road and Stowupland Street. After the coming of the Gipping Navigation in 1793 and the railway in 1846, several inns and beerhouses opened around the river & railway area. The establishment of beerhouses was encouraged by the 1830 Beer Act, which enabled a householder to sell beer from their premises on the payment of 42 shillings for a licence. From then on the number of these establishments increased, many of these such as the Unicorn and the Royal William are still with us today having eventually gained full licences. By the early 20th century largely through pressure from the Temperance movement, the government of the day felt that the number of these small beerhouses was encouraging drunkenness, and the conditions for renewal of licences became more strict, therefore establishments had to justify their existence and many were closed.

The Names of Inns

The name of an Inn originated from its sign, which would be displayed outside. In an age when few could read, these were an aid to recognition. In larger towns and cities not only inns but also other trading premises and shops would have signs, eventually inns were the only establishments (after 1761) which were allowed to display a sign. On larger premises these could be very elaborate, sometimes spanning the road. The most notable of these "gallows signs" was probably at The Scole Inn near Diss. Stonham Magpie retains its sign which spans the A140 to this day.

Many early inns that dated from mediaeval times would have been associated with the church or monastery, these had signs of a religious significance; the Angel seems to be the only example in Stowmarket. Later heraldry was also a big influence, we think of the White Hart and Red Lion. Most inn names in town have no special local significance; a few such as the Barge alongside the River Gipping give a clue as to their origins.

The Role of Women in Innkeeping

As mentioned above brewing and serving beer had once been seen as a woman's work. Their role in brewing seems to have ceased as brewing became more of a business and less of a domestic task. This role is often hidden in the official records by the fact that with the introduction of licensing a man's name would usually appear as the official licensee. A married woman was not legally responsible as her property belonged to her husband while they were married. However the day to day running of the establishment was usually the role of the wife and/or daughters. Only when a man died did his widow appear as the licensee, even then she would often remarry and the new husband would then appear as the licensee. This is also evidenced by the fact that a man would often have another occupation such as butcher or blacksmith which could be carried out on the premises. No doubt he would be called in at busy times or to deal with any troublesome customers, although many of the woman were probably quite capable of dealing with this too!

9

Brewing In Stowmarket

At one time each establishment would have had it's own brewhouse and supplied it's own needs. The first individual in Stowmarket to start brewing on a larger scale seems to have been William Bunn, who combined brewing with his other occupation as an apothecary. He acquired a few inns in and around Stowmarket and passed these on to his son-in-law William Aldrich in 1750. Members of the Aldrich family added to this estate by acquiring even more inns in and around town. In 1805, a later William Aldrich had to hand all this property over to his father-in-law John Cobbold the Ipswich brewer in lieu of a debt of £12,000. Naturally, Cobbold supplied these with his own beer, but several smaller breweries were established in the town throughout the 19th century.

The last small local brewer to brew on the premises was probably George Diaper, who established the Crown Brewery at the Rose and Crown in Bridge Street in the 1880s. Beer was brewed at The Stag Tavern for a very short period in 2001.

Many of the buildings described here have a long and interesting existence both before and after their lives as inns and beerhouses, brief details have been included. Establishments that can be termed as clubs such as the Riverside Club and Jokers have not been included in this survey.

The authors have been researching the subject for some 18 years and have amassed more information than can be included here, indeed some of the premises could almost warrant a small book on their own!

Stowmarket saw its number of pubs peak in the second half of the 19th century, followed by a slow decline. There has been some good news though, The Stag in Bury Street opened in 1982 and remains a lively pub, and even as this book goes to press the opening of a new Kings Arms is imminent, this will be in the same building in Station Approach as that pub that closed some 50 years ago.

ANGEL/GREYHOUND
Corner of Tavern Street and Market Place
pre 1524 - 1982

Angel - Greyhound

The Angel, as well as coming first on an alphabetical list of Stowmarket inns, has probably the longest continuous or near continuous use as an inn in the town, under both this name and it's later name of the Greyhound.

The building which had in the 1970s being listed as of 17th century construction, has in recent years been investigated by an expert in timber framed buildings who has found that at least part of the building dates back to the late 14th century making it one of the oldest if not the oldest building in the town other than the parish church.

The name of the inn with it's religious connotation would suggest a Pre-Reformation origin and the first record of an inn of this name in the town is in 1524 when in his will a Thomas Benson left the Angel to his wife Johan.

In 1547 lands and revenues of all foundations that had been endowed to benefit the souls of their founders were appropriated to the Crown. An investigation in 1578 to find property that had not been declared mentions "The Angel held by one Gifford being formally held to use

11

of a priest to say a mass in Stowmarket Church" but that "John Wage the elder did will them to leave out the said lands". This may have been a mass for the soul of a previous owner of the Angel, maybe John Wage and would have been stipulated in a will, but we have no record of this. The mass was known as "Bils Masse" and the priest was named as Sir Giles Wells. There may be a connection here with an area of charity land in the town that was known as Bills which was left to the parish by a John Wage.

In 1679 "a Souldger died at Angle" a fatality from an epidemic, probably of smallpox, which spread through the company, billeted in the town at the time. From at least the time of the ownership of William Bunn in 1734 there was a malting in the Angel Yard and also a brewing house, this lasted through the Aldrich ownership, possibly the beer for the other pubs owned by this family in and around the town was brewed here.

When the name of the Angel was changed to the Greyhound it was taking over the name of another ancient inn, this had stood on the other side of Tavern Street and had recently closed and was in the same ownership. [See the Greyhound, Tavern Street].

One family with a long connection with the Greyhound was the Hudgell family, two Jonathan Hudgell's, father and son were here from at least 1810 to 1841, Jonathan the elder was born in 1758 in Claydon, he married Ann Bowles in 1788 in Gipping. Their son Jonathan was born in 1791 and married his cousin Temperance Hudgell. Jonathan the elder died in 1821 and in his will left his "wines liquors and provision" to his widow. Jonathan the younger took over the inn on his father's death but he also worked as a saddle and harness maker as his father had. In 1841 or soon after the family left the inn and Stowmarket for Cockfield where Jonathan continued this trade. NL

Owners of Angel

1???-1524	Tomas Benson
1524-15??	John Benson
15??-1547	John Wage the elder ?
1620-1643	Philemon Dixon

1643-1673	Elizabeth Draper/Humphrey Wheatly/Philemon Broom ?
1673-1687	John Broom, worsted weaver
1687-1691	Thomas Love of Combs, mortgaged to John Eldred of Bury St. Edmunds
1691-1712	John Eldred of Bury St Edmunds
1712-1715	Ann and Thomas Eldred, widow and son of John executors of Johns Eldred's will
1715-1734	Argor Catchpole, son in law of Ann Eldred buys from her for £145
1734-1734	Judith and Thomas Catchpole daughter in law and grandson of Argor
1734-1750	William Bunn
1750-1762	William Aldrich, son in law of William Bunn
1762-1768	Pelham Aldrich, son of William
1768-1797	John Aldrich
1797-1802	Rev William Aldrich and John Aldrich, nephew and son of John Aldrich
1805	John Aldrich mortgages Angel to John Cobbold brewer of Ipswich

Owners of Greyhound

1810	John Aldrich sells the Angel now called the Greyhound to John Cobbold
1810	John Cobbold brewer

Occupiers of Angel

1578-1588	[Phillip?] Gifford
1673-1691	Humphrey Wheatley
1695-1718	Andrew Spence
1718-1726	John Smith
1728-1735	Thomas Birch/Burch previously at Flowerpot and later at White Horse
1735-1742	William Claxson/Claxton

1742-1760	Hezekiah Poole/Pooley
1760-1764	John Witham junior
1767-1798	James Payne, member of Stow Hundred Volunteers, buried "with military honours amidst a vast concourse of spectators"
1805.1805	John Aldrich

Occupiers of Greyhound

1805-1821	Jonathan Hudgell senior
1821-1841	Jonathan Hudgell junior
1841-1850	John Dixon Taylor, carpenter
1851-1851	William Wood
1851-1852	Robert Turrell
1852-1870	Leonard Myall
1871-1880	Robert G. Parker, then to White Horse, son Oliver later at Unicorn & Royal Oak
1880-1892	Abraham Last
1892-1893	Mrs. Sarah Last
1893-1896	Frederick William Leathers, Messrs Ranson's dray smashed into window 1894
1896-1904	Harry C. Mulley, fire in yard 1901
1904-1910	William Chinery, town mortuary situated in yard c.1904
1910-1913	Joseph Arthur Oliver, then to Queens Head
1913-1937	John Ernest William Haggar, then to Dukes Head & founder of Stowmarket Mineral Water Co.
1938-1945	Thomas Walter Clarkson
1945-1957	Harry Walter Edwards, Mrs Edwards worked in Burrows fruit and veg shop
1957-1966	William Victor Edwards
1966-1969	Anna E. Edwards
1969-1982	Frank W. & Jean M. Cann, Frank worked at Eastern Electricity
Nov 1982	Closed

BAKERS ARMS
56 Violet Hill (now Fairfield Hill)
pre 1836 - 1913

The beerhouse known as the Bakers Arms occupied a house in what is now Fairfield Hill. As would be expected from it's name the beerhouse shared the premises with a bakery, it was also the home of Richard Ayliffe described as a baker in the 1851 census. The owner of the property from at least 1836 until 1858 was John George Hart.

Hart had come to Stowmarket as manager of the town's branch of Oakes and Co. Bury St. Edmunds bank, taking over this role from his brother-in-law Thomas Gross. Over the years Hart had amassed a considerable amount of property and was active in many aspects of the town's life, he was said to be well respected and lived plainly but to have embarked on various speculations. On his death in 1861 it was revealed that he had used the capital of the bank for these speculations. He also left the administration of the town charities, for which he had been responsible in his role as churchwarden in considerable disarray, prompting the Charity Commissioners to review the entire running of all the town charities.

The premises were offered for sale at the Fox on 15th September 1856 being purchased by Philips Brothers of Stowmarket Brewery.

Richard Ayliffe had been succeeded by George Fiske and then Charles Lillistone, the bakery side of the enterprise continuing. Charles Lillistone seems to have also used the premises as a lodging house, as in the 1871 census 20 are listed there!

The Bakers Arms was sold by F. B. Marriott for £310 in 1865. From 1867 to 1886 it was owned by Charles Wood of Bacton Brewery before being purchased with an adjoining cottage for £610 by King & Son brewers of Bury St. Edmunds, (who were to join with that towns other major brewer the following year to become Greene King).

Frederick Barnard previously of the Staff Of Life took over the running of the beerhouse in 1879 before moving to the Horse And Groom in 1883. Barnard continued to bake on the premises, but conditions cannot have been the most hygienic as he was reported to have refused to pay seven shillings for the removal of "night soil". Two years later this and another nearby lodging house were closed temporarily and disinfected due to a smallpox outbreak.

The next few years saw a few temporary landlords, then came Charles Lillistone junior son of a previous tenant. Sarah Anne Ward and her son Phillip from the Vulcan Arms arrived in 1896. With so many lodgers coming and going it was not surprising that trouble would break out from time to time and Phillip is reported to have had to call the police once when gypsies were fighting in the yard. Phillip Ward himself met a tragic end when he fell downstairs, breaking his neck. His widow then remarried, to Thomas Naylor. As Annie Naylor she continued to take lodgers and bake, for sixpence she would cook Sunday dinners in the bread oven and deliver them. Her husband however drunk the profits and they moved to Ipswich in 1909. Her successor was the same Frederick Barnard who had been in occupation some 25 years previously, ending his long career as a licence holder in 1912.

The final licensee was Arthur Oscar Oliver, but the move to reduce the number of beerhouses meant that the renewal of the licence was refused in 1913, the amount of £548 being paid to Greene King as compensation and £60 to the tenant.

After this Arthur Oliver carried on running the premises as a lodging house. A fire occurred on the 21st May 1914, the cause being an oil lamp that the housekeeper Caroline Douglas was carrying as she climbed a ladder to her attic bedroom, she consquently lost her life in the fire.

Along with the other houses in the street the building was demolished in 1986. NL

Occupiers

1836-1851	Richard Ayliffe
1851-1853	George Fiske, a baker, fined 40s in 1853 for opening before time on a Sunday
1853-1879	Charles Lillistone, fined 1858, (the owners/occupiers have a right of way to Bury Street, 1862)
1879-1883	Frederick Barnard
1883-1883	William Hubbard
1883-1884	Charles Chandler
1884-1895	Charles Lillistone jnr.
1895-1896	Emily Lillistone
1896-1901	Sarah Ann Ward
1901-1906	Phillip Ward (fined 1899 for being in charge of an infected child, scarlet fever)
1906-1909	Annie Elizabeth Naylor
1909-1912	Frederick Barnard
1912-1913	Arthur Oscar Oliver. A fire in 1914 caused the death of lodger Caroline Douglas.

BAKERS ARMS
Combs Ford
c.1842 - c1885

After closure 1906

Positioned nearly opposite the Gladstone Arms, and almost next door to the long established Magpie Inn this beerhouse was never going to thrive but it did last almost half a century. Like many small bakers of the period people used the left over yeast to brew beer, Thomas Mayhew and Mary his wife ran the business and in addition had a small shop to boost their income. After the death of her husband in c1845 Mary continued with the business until her son William took over. William had several brushes with the law viz: 1859 charged with assault, fined 10 shillings, 1860 fined 20 shillings for keeping open after hours and again in 1862 for a similar offence fined £5 (£337); apparently he had had many convictions for short weight in the past. He passed away in 1870 aged just 45 years. The next landlord was David Brett, who in 1873 had three panes of glass broken by vandals; his age was given as 39. In 1876 like his predecessor he too was fined for opening out of hours. By 1877 the licence was transferred to Roger Bird who stayed until 1881. Baker James Mulley was in residence until c1884, in March 1885 an advert' appeared in the Ipswich Journal "For sale at the Fox, a beerhouse, bakehouse, and bake office and two cottages in occupation of James Mulley" the sale was withdrawn at £190 (£14,700). Again in 1885 the paper carried another advert' for the sale of the beerhouse "Lately James Mulley, has been unoccupied for over twelve months, Mulley would not go into the house", strangely though the licence was renewed.

Some ten years after it's closure this beautiful 15th century? building was very nearly lost due to a serious fire, the four dilapidated cottages almost adjoining were totally destroyed, and the fire brigade could only just contain the ravaging fire. Repaired, the building once more became just a shop and newsagents and was at one time owned by the ex manager of Ipswich Town Football Club Sir Bobby Robson. BAS

Occupiers
1842-1844   Thomas Mayhew
1846-1855   Mary Mayhew
1858-1870   William Mayhew
1870-1877   David Brett
1877-1881   Roger Bird
1881-1885   James Mulley

BARGE
18 Stowupland Street
pre 1805 - 1909

After closure

"4d could get a pie, a pint and a thick ear at the Barge"
[local saying in 1900]

The names of some pubs tell the story of their origin. The Barge backing onto the River Gipping owes it's origins to the Stowmarket to Ipswich Navigation opened for use in 1793. It was first mentioned in deeds of 1805, when it was included in the pubs handed over by John Aldrich to his father-in-law John Cobbold, brewer of Ipswich in lieu of debts. So it can be said that it's origins were closely associated with the navigation. Situated as it was near the head of navigation it must have been a welcome sight to the bargees as they completed their journey from Ipswich. Run from at least 1810 until 1842 by one George Codd at which date he moved to the nearby Wagon And Horses. He was succeeded by John Bird. There is some evidence that Bird may have also been a brewer.

Navigation between Stowmarket and Ipswich was suggested as early as 1719. It's opening in 1793 marked a new phase in the town's life. Enterprising businessmen came to the town around this time, such as Manning Prentice from Bungay, a man who soon made himself useful in the business, religious, and social life of the town. The Lankesters from Essex brought their wine & spirit trade. Both Prentice and Lankester were adherents of the Independent Meeting House and on their arrival they set about building up the church which was at that time at a low ebb. Heavy industry arrived in 1812 with James Wood's ironworks.

Within not much more than a generation the Navigation was overtaken by the arrival of the railway in 1846. The concern was at that time bought by the Eastern Union Railway Company, it was all downhill from then on as the river trade diminished, losing out to the railway which followed the river along the Gipping valley to Ipswich.

By 1865 a William Ruffell was in residence and was fined in that year for raffling, he was also a blacksmith, a reminder that publican was rarely the sole trade of the licensee. It is probable that in many cases although a man's name appears on the licence it was his wife who actually took care of the day to day running of the pub. A woman is rarely listed as the licensee unless she had been widowed and the licence transferred to her name. In 1871 William married Caroline Glasspole of the White Horse Station Road less than 6 months after the death of her husband George, the Ruffells may have run that establishment for a short time as an Alfred Burman appears at the Barge from 1870 to 1872. Ruffell may have carried on his blacksmith work at the Barge throughout this time as he was back as licensee there by the end of 1873, and being fined 10 shillings for allowing out of hours drinking in 1885. His wife Caroline had been previously married 3 times, she brought 3 daughters from her first marriage as well as 2 sisters to the household. William Ruffell stayed on until his death in 1888. Caroline and her children then moved to Sudbury. Ruffell was succeeded by Thomas Makens; he was fined for keeping 5 dogs with only a licence for 2 in 1890. Thomas had used the dogs when he worked as a drover. When the dogs died Thomas had them stuffed and sat them on each side of his fireplace!

The lifespan of the Barge pub matched the useful life of the navigation, closing in 1909, still in the hands of Cobbold's, £359.9.0. was paid as compensation for the loss of trade. The last occupier was Edgar Chenery who was tenant from 1895 until closure. Chenery continued to rent the premises until March 1910 when it was sold to G.A. Woodward. The premises are now "Louises" a ladies hairdresser. NL

<u>Owners</u>
Before 1805   John Aldrich
1805-1910   Cobbolds

<u>Occupiers</u>
1810-1842   George Codd
1842-1851   John Bird
1852-1853   John Hart
1853-1855   John Smith
1855-1855   John Bird
1856-1856   William Malyon & wife Mary, he was a fish
               curer/monger
1858-1858   John Goodswen
1860-1863   Elleana Goodswen
1863-1866   William Malyon
1866-1870   William Ruffell
1871-1873   Alfred Burman
1873-1888   William Ruffell, 1885 fined for selling out of
               hours
1880-1880   George Ralph - interim licence
1888-1895   Thomas Makens/Makings
1895-1909   Edgar Chenery

BELL
Combs unknown location

The only known reference to this is from Suffolk JP Devereux Edgar's notebook & states that Henry Martin was there in May 1711. Martin probably went to the Combs Magpie before 1717. BAS

BELL
Bury Street, location unknown
c.1732 - c1800

Jeremiah Bigsby jnr, owner of the Bell made his will in 1734 and died in 1736 leaving the premises & orchard to his wife Elizabeth during her lifetime, & afterwards to his son James. In the next will that has been found the owner Jeremiah Bigsby leaves the property to his half sister Alice, the wife of Chess Stedman, this Jeremiah died in 1747. Alice passed away in 1752, her widowed husband Chess advertised the pub' to let in 1758. In 1782 Chess himself died, the pub' was advertised for sale "a freehold well accustomed public house now in the several tenures of Abraham Salmon (landlord) & John Tansy, consisting 2 low rooms in front, a large parlour, 4 chambers, good cellar, brewhouse, stables, about 3 acres good garden, moderate land tax & no lease". Thomas Rust was the owner before 1797, and by December the following year John Edgar Rust was the owner. A court roll of 1814 confirms Elizabeth Peirson as the owner but by then the Bell had long since closed. BAS

1732-1741	Thomas Thompson occupier
1742-1748	Anthony Allom, to the Black Swan
1748-1749	William Stebing paid poor rate?
1749-1751+	John Smith/Smyth paid poor rate?
1758	to let
1777	timber sale
1781	Lost bay horse 15 hands apply Edmund Baldwin
before 1782	Abraham Salmon, he died 1792
1792-1799	Mary Salmon widow of Abraham (died 1804)
1800	Distress furniture sale
1804	Reference to leathering the pump by the Bell
1814	Reference to a stable in the Bell yard.

BELL INN
16 Bury Road
c.1836 – c.1919

c.1913

On the corner of Sickhouse Lane (now Pound Lane) & Bury Road is a detached house, James Woods the local entrepreneur & owner of the Suffolk Iron Works in Bury Street built this. He was however made bankrupt just a few months after completion of the house, & his executors were running the pub by 1838. In 1822 Elizabeth the daughter of James Woods had married Robert Paul and by 1839 Robert & Francis Paul were running the property. They also owned the Unicorn Brewery in Foundation Street Ipswich, and kept the Bell just one year until local bank Oakes/Bevan/Moor & Bevan headed by their manager John George Hart acquired the business; they owned it until 1874. Meanwhile the Unicorn Brewery sold off the un-expired part of their lease in 1842. From 1874 until 1896 the Bell was owned by brewer William Golland Ranson of Violet Hill Stowmarket, he owned many pubs in the local area and was also a maltster & coal merchant. An amusing piece from a newspaper of 1880 states "a few days ago a gentleman from London visited the landlord Mr Aldous of the Blue Bell (sic) and sold him a donkey for £50. The animal is said to be capable of accomplishing one mile in three & half minutes.

The long-eared creature created quite a sensation at the railway station when he was elevated into a horsebox". John Aldous was hurt in an accident in 1881; he passed away on January 28th 1894 aged 53. His housekeeper Miss Mckay died an hour before his funeral on Wednesday January 31st.

The Bell was put up for sale in 1896 "a bar with bay 16 x 12 ft, tap room 18 x 15 feet, sitting room, kitchen, storeroom, wash-house, cellar, landing, 6 bedrooms, wood shed, outhouse, & a pump & well, timber 6 stall stable with loft over, range of lean-to loose boxes with pigsty, cart shed, enclosed gig & harness house, rent £20 p.a." Tollemache & Co became the final owners in 1896 & put the Bell up for sale in 1919. BAS

1836-1836	William Tricker
1838-1839	William Farrow
1839	John Burton
1839-1840	John Broom, to Pot of Flowers then Carpenters Arms
1840-1841	Peter Trew jnr, a 25 year old carpenter in 1841 (see Pot Of Flowers 1814 his father)
1842-1848	William Turner, a butcher
1848-1876	Joseph Dade, butcher age 39 in 1851, stood surety for Edmund Stott Barnard
1876-1894	John Aldous, horse dealer age 40 in 1881
1894	Frederick Sage
1895	Alexander Higgins
1895	Frederick W Lemmon
1896-1904	Thomas Martin, horse dispute 1900, his son fined 1903, Thomas buried 1904 age 47
1904-1919	Mrs Georgina Martin aged 60, married John Welham 1919
1919	For sale late the Bell, late tenant Mrs W Ward claims counters, beer engine etc, sold to Mrs Jarred of Wretten Norfolk £490.

BLACK LION
Stowmarket, unknown location

Stowupland churchwarden's accounts for April 1625 "paid out for bread and beare (beer) at Langumes". Anne Langham inn licence 1617 £5, and 1618 ten shillings rent, and 1620 rent ten shillings but paid only five. This rent information comes from the notebook of Sir Gyles Mompesson. That is all we know of this inn, it may be that it was known by another name. BAS

BLACK SWAN/SWAN
Crowe Street
c.1658 - c.1818 [renamed White Hart]

In 1681 Peter Brasier, apothecary, left the Black Swan to his daughter Mary Cross, his will also mentions new stables. Peter is likely to have owned the inn in 1662 when he supplied soldiers in the town with beer and other items. As far back as 1658 he had issued a farthing trade token. From 1677 to 1685 the tenant was John Blakes, and after his death it was ran by his widow Elizabeth. John Watts succeeded her; he was there for 28 years. By this time the owner was Daniel Thorpe, and from 1715 he was the occupier as well. On his death in 1748, his second wife Dinah ran the inn before disposing of it to Robert Marriott of Thorney Hall Stowupland. A succession of tenants appears over the next 20 years or so.

Robert Marriott passed the ownership on to his eldest nephew John Marriott.An advertisement in the Ipswich Journal offering the inn to let in 1790 describes it thus –
"The premises called the Swan near the Market Place, which consists of good cellars, kitchen, parlour, bar-room, pantry, backhouse, brewing office, chambers and garrets, yard and stables. All in good repair"

The fact that it was advertised again in 1796 "at an easy rent" may indicate that the Swan was losing out to competition from the other inns around the market place, certainly by 1801 the late tenant John Jeffree was selling his entire household furniture and effects.
The year 1802 saw the appearance of Henry Ungless at the Swan; he

would play a prominent part at various inns in the town over the next 30 years. Ungless was born in Laxfield about 1777, the son of Henry, a butcher and his wife Frances. Henry junior married Sarah Tombline in 1797 at St George's Hanover Square London. A daughter Frances was baptised at St James Church Soho in 1799. However in October 1802 Henry announced his arrival at the Swan in Stowmarket, in a notice in the local press stating that he had "laid in a good assortment of Neat Old Wines and foreign spirits" as well as offering dinners on market day and good stabling. He didn't stay here long, by January 1804 he was at the Pot Of Flowers in Bury Street. He did however return to the Swan in a few years time under its new name of the White Hart. From 1804 to 1818 John Cuthbert was tenant but his main occupation was a butcher, no doubt Mrs Cuthbert saw to the day to day running of the inn. The last mention of the inn under this name was in April 1816, and at sometime after this it was renamed the White Hart. NL

Owners
1658-1681	Peter Brasier
1681	Mary Cross
17??-1748	Daniel Thorpe
1748-1750	Dinah Thorpe
1750-1763	Robert Marriott, Solicitor of Thorney Hall
17??-1799	John Marriott, eldest nephew of Robert

Occupiers
1677-1685	John Blakes
1685-1686	Elizabeth Blakes, second wife of John
1686-1714	John Watts
1714-1715	Richard Southgate
1715-1748	Daniel Thorpe
1748-1750	Dinah Thorpe widow
1750-1751	Anthony Allum
1760-1761	John Elmer
1764-1764	John Baker
1767-1783	James Raffe, bankrupt 1782
1796-1797	Robert Clarke
1798-1801	John Jeffree
1802-1804	Henry Ungless
1804-1818	John Cuthbert

BLUE POSTS
Stowupland Street/4 Station Road
c.1839 - 1941

c.1907   *c.1971 after closure*

In 1853 James Diaper a 39 year old wine, spirit, & porter merchant (Guinness, is a type of porter) thanked the people of the town for their patronage over the last 14 years & reminded his clientele that they could purchase Allsops pale ale, Guinness as well as brandy etc from him. Thus we are able to ascertain a possible starting date for the liquor store that was to become the Blue Posts. Apparently blue posts were used originally to mark the boundary of sporting lands used for hunting. Situated in a prominent position, as was often the case, this building is constructed of wattle & daub. It originally had a front entrance facing Station Road, but was altered to an angled corner entrance at some undetermined date before 1935; the facing tiles would seem to be an Edwardian addition. There never was a sign, just the name painted on the window glass. In 1861 Diaper sold out to brothers Thomas and Jubal Raffe, they were journeymen millers & corn merchants, their family operated a small shop in Combs. Jubal came to Stowmarket with his wife Ellen and children and settled in the California (Lime Tree Place?) part of town. By 1871 the family of seven children had moved to Ipswich Road just opposite the present

28

Regal cinema, tragically his wife Ellen died in 1872 aged just 39 years, later Jubal remarried. Thomas Raffe lived at the liquor store and in 1871 was described as a wine and spirit merchant, a farmer of 90 acres employing 4 men & a boy; he died in December 1877 at only 53 years of age.

An application was made in January 1878 on behalf of the trustees of Thomas Raffe for Messrs Andrews & Tidmarsh for a licence to sell on the premises etc, this was granted to accountant Joseph Andrews of 7 Ironmongers Lane London for the benefit of the creditors. The Ipswich Journal of April 1878 has an advertisement for the sale of the business including 3 residences, shops etc. The rate books for the next few months are blank, but by June 1878 Alexander Clutterbuck trading as the Stowmarket Brewery (this firm's history is told elsewhere) purchased the premises for £2,800, (£195,000) & in November 1878 an interim licence was granted to Mr Wilson from Clutterbuck's. The census of 1881 shows that Emily Raffe the 60 year widow of Thomas was still at the property & acting as housekeeper to barman Robert Lewis, her brother in law Jubal was a commercial traveller still in the wine & spirit business.

July 1882 saw the premises sold to the expanding empire of Edward Greene of Bury St Edmunds; this firm in turn became Green, King in June 1887. Successions of barmen/managers looked after the pub, here are a few gleanings from local newspapers & first hand accounts. In 1884 the closing time was extended from 10 p.m. until 11 p.m. & in 1900 a six-day licence was agreed. A new upstairs room was renovated in 1926, this was used among other things to house the Thursday evening meetings of the Ancient Order of Buffalos, the slip was down steps in Church Walk, the snug was accessed via the corner door & the main bar was in Station Road. Manager Arthur Ernest Shackell in 1935 won about £200 (some £10,000 today) on the pools & promptly decided to retire.

On Thursday February 6th 1941 Charlie Codd, cycle dealer of Station Road, was in the Blue Post's parlour with his two sons Vivian & Ivan & friends Mr & Mrs Jack Farrow, suddenly, the siren sounded an imminent air raid, machine gunfire was heard, everyone threw themselves on the floor & heard the bullets hit the Water Works opposite. Some years later a bullet hole was found in the weather vane on the church spire, this may well have come from this incident.

The licence was surrendered by letter dated April 30th 1941, & the Blue Posts with the adjoining numbers 6 & 8 Station Road were sold. Many small trades occupied the premises over the next 60 years, including an accessory shop of O. G. Barnard the local garage. In 2002 the corner doorway was blocked up & the building was converted to residential use. BAS

Managers etc:

1881-1887	Robert Arthur Lewis
1887-1888	Fritz H A Gustavel
1889-1892	John F Howard, age 33 in 1891
1892-1900	James Betteridge
1900-1911	Frederick William Simper
1911-1914	James Maulkin King, licence transfer King to Simper 14/1/1914
1914-1917	Frederick William Simper again
1917-1925	Robert George Balls, burial Alice Balls age 55 in 1925
1925-1935	Arthur Ernest Shackell
1936-1937	Phil Willis
1938-1941	Alexander Davis

BULL
Market Place
pre 1714 – 1809

After closure

The Bull stood on the site that many will remember as Stearns the chemist, it is currently a mobile phone shop and a florist situated between the Buttermarket and Station Road, possibly Bucks estate agents was also part of the Bull.

Bull Lane was a name used for the thoroughfare now known as Station Road. An even earlier name for this way recorded in manorial records is Dolphin Lane, prompting the thought that maybe an earlier name for the Bull could have been the Dolphin, however no other record of an inn of that name has been found.

Although the Bull occupied a prominent position in the Market Place relatively little is known about it's origins. The first record of it is in 1714 when it appears in a list of licensed premises in the notebook of Devereaux Edgar, as a justice of the peace he was responsible for issuing licences to sell beer and spirits, but the inn almost certainly dated from before then. At that time a Samuel Langham was the licensee and the family seem to have owned the Bull from at least 1732 to 1785.

In 1732 the Bull was advertised to let as "an old accustomed house, brews it's own beer, near Market Place, good cellar and stable." suggesting that it had been established for some time. The stable cannot have been that large as the site today is quite restricted, however it is worth bearing in mind that the thoroughfare to the north would probably have been much narrower then. There are still cellars under the present building and these may well be the original cellars of the Bull.

The William Langham who owned it later in the 18th century was also a butcher. Several advertisements appeared in the Ipswich Journal offering the Bull to let around 1785 and by 1798 the Bull had come into the hands of John Cobbold the Ipswich brewer and seems to have been one of the first inns he owned in Stowmarket.

On his death in 1804 a Mr. James Frewer was described as – "master of the Bull Inn Stowmarket".

In 1809 William Bristo took the inn but in September 1809 it was being announced in the press that it was to become a private house. For some time the house continued to be known as the Old Bull and the site as Bull Corner.
The will of Richard Freeman 1829 suggests that he bought the building in 1809, described as "being in Cloth Market Lane being the premises late belonging to the Bull Inn now converted into a cabinet makers shop. On the north part on the Kings Highway leading from Ipswich to Bury on the West part whereon the market of Stowmarket is now kept and whereon the flesh stalls and butchers shambles formerly stood"

The old building was demolished about 1843. Thomas Simpson, a pharmacist who had traded in the town from 1833 transferred his business to the new building on the site. Next door at the house now Bucks estate agent lived Spencer Freeman surgeon, having been left this building and the former Bull by his father Richard. Spencer Freeman was related by marriage to Thomas Simpson and it is likely that Freeman was responsible for the rebuilding on the Bull site for Thomas Simpson. The chemist business continued, being later known as Stearns until it closed in 1992. NL

Owners

before 1714 to 1772	Samuel?, then John, then William, then Jane Langham
1772 to 1785	John Green of Combs
1785	William Brook part owner?
1798	John Cobbold
1809	Richard Freeman

Occupiers

before-1714	Samuel Langham
1714-1716	Charles Woods junior
1716-1717	Sarah Woods, widow
1717-1719	Jeremiah Bigsby
1732-1742	William Langham
1742-1746	Mary Taylor, widow
1754-1783	William Mills, previously at the Hat and Feathers
1783-1785	Richard Alkin, later at Woolpit Swan
1785-1790	Mr. Rumley
1791-1804	James Frewer, plumber, glazier & painter
1807-1809	William Bristo

BURY STREET BEERHOUSE
Bury Street Stowmarket

A guess at the location of this beerhouse would be on the left hand-side going to Bury St Edmunds, and just before where lower Violet Hill joins Bury Street. In 1837 Henry Ungless Jnr was the occupier, with no evidence of beerhouse, however his father was involved in the Black Swan, Pot of Flowers and the White Hart. In 1838 the occupier was John Wells a beer-seller and a Mrs Fenton (Ann?) the owner. By 1839 John Burton (from the Bell?) was the occupier and Mrs Fenton still owned the property. BAS

CARDINALS ROAD BEERHOUSE
68 Cardinals Road
c1853 - 1864

Philip Barnard born c1818 was the only landlord; he was also a platelayer on the railway. His Shelland born wife Charlotte carried out the day to day running of the beerhouse, and by 1861 there were seven children to look after. In 1855 it was described as Gipping Street beerhouse and in 1859 as a shop/beerhouse. This family of Barnards completely disappears from the town in about 1864.

The owner was a Mr Fox, the 1861 census informs of two possible candidates, Richard Fox age 40 a Bury Street chandler and Edward Fox a 59 year old engineer of Stowupland Street. BAS

CARPENTERS ARMS
Bury Street
c.1836 – 1868

1868

George Goodwin was the first known owner, followed by a Lockwood and finally Jonathan Godbold and his executors. The 1836 rate books inform us that William Horrox lived at this address, whether this was a beerhouse at this time is unknown, but it is very probable. Certainly by September 1837 this was a beerhouse and the landlord was Lewis Cuthbert, his tenancy finished in 1840 when Alfred Field took over. In January 1842 Jonathan Godbold a CARPENTER had arrived, and it's most likely that it was he who gave the beerhouse it's name, he also purchased the property at some time around 1850. The landlords then followed the usual short tenancy theme. The infamous Bury Street fire of July 12th 1868 finally destroyed the Carpenters Arms, along with several other houses leaving many families homeless; a local poem exists regarding the catastrophe. BAS

Owners
c1832-1848   George Goodwin of Coddenham
1849-1850   Lockwood owner
1851-1868   Jonathan Godbold & executors, aged 42 in 1851

Occupiers

1836	William Horrox if a beerhouse
1836-1837	William Felgate if a beerhouse
1837-1840	Lewis Cuthbert
1840-1841	Alfred Field
1842-1852	Jonathan Godbold
1853-1854	James Fairweather
c1855-1856	Samuel Ramsey
1856-1860	John Broom, to Pot of Flowers
1860-1863	Robert Barker a miller age 42 in 1861
1863-1865	Robert Pryke
1865-1868	James Adams to Royal William.

CHERRY TREE
Bury Street (near the Stag)
c.1779 – 1807

Duffield Offord was the probable owner until 1782, his son James may have been the next owner until 1793 when George Holden followed him (see his story elsewhere), by 1805 George was in the Ipswich goal for debt. Richard Crawley an Ipswich wine merchant had a lease for the Cherry Tree and four houses in 1805, also involved was Thomas Rout of Stowmarket. A document of 1806 shows John Kent with a lease for one year of the Cherry Tree and it's yard and garden in Haughley Street (Bury Street). Holdens 1811 directory has Richard R Crawley wine merchant. BAS

CHURCH YARD BEERHOUSE
c.1849 – 1863

John Day was born in London in 1793, by 1823 he was living in Stowmarket with his wife Mary who was pregnant with their first child William George. John was to spend the rest of his life in town at Elm House No 6 Church Yard, this substantial house was built c1780, it faced Station Road and was converted into two dwellings sometime before 1912, and was demolished c1948. John was a leather dresser/shoemaker and conducted his business in what was until January 2009 Hayward's Solicitors building in the Butter Market. Some three years after his wife had passed away he married Ann Philips from Nayland in Essex, she assisted him in the business as a shoe binder, as did their only daughter Sarah. They had five children together, their first son Charles Philip Day was apprenticed to tailor W G Balls in Union Street, the two other sons were apprenticed to coach builder Samuel Bridges in Tavern Street, now Stannards Electrical.

By about 1849 John, as well as his shoemaking business started his brewing concern, he brewed the beer at the bottom of his garden, in a shed just large enough for one or two people, a pipe conveyed the beer to the cellar in Elm House where it was stored. The small brewery was still standing in 1916, situated near two pear trees.

John attended morning services at the Friar Street Unitarian Chapel in Ipswich. A train took him there in the mornings & after remaining for the evening services he would walk the 12 miles back home to Stowmarket!. John passed away in June 1863 aged 70 years.

For more on this family see the Stowmarket Post for March 3rd 1916, including the nostalgic return to Stowmarket of the three sons. BAS

COCK
Combs, location unknown

1607 and 1616 an Alehouse in Combs, 1617 Richard Edgar inn licence £5, 1618 and 1620 ditto at 10 shillings per annum. Five pounds in 1618 equates to about £ 800 in 2009. BAS

COCK AND PYE
Stowmarket, location unknown

In 1733 Charles Colson paid the poor rate, and in late 1733 and 1734 it was paid by William Bunn. Judging by the amount paid £4 (£600 in 2009) it was about half the size of the Rose (£10). BAS

CROWN
Bury Street
pre 1618 – [& after 1755 renamed Fox & Hounds]

Although the first definite record of this inn is in 1624, there is some evidence that it could have been in existence earlier, possibly as early as 1562, it seems to have been in the Wage family at this earlier date although if it was then an inn is not known.

The first mention of the inn by name is in 1624 when John Wage left the Crown to his wife Anne in his will. An earlier John Wage in 1562 had left a copyhold dwelling to his wife Cecily and after her death to their son John. The suppositions being that these 2 Johns were father and son or grandfather and grandson. A John Wage was certainly recorded as an innholder in 1618 and 1619 but his inn was not named.

The inn eventually came to William Wage, the son of John and Anne on Anne's death. The Crown remained in the hands of the Wage family until about 1680. The family seems to have also run the inn themselves, as there are no records of any tenants.

One infamous guest at the Crown was Matthew Hopkins of Manningtree in Essex in 1645, or the Witchfinder General as he styled himself. "A rate for the discovery of witches" was levied on the inhabitants and the sum of £23.0s.6d was raised for the purpose. Several witches are said to have been discovered and a Mary Fuller of Combs is recorded as among the "witches" hung at Bury St. Edmunds that year. Hopkins also visited Rattlesden and Bacton. William Wage was paid nine shillings and six pence by the churchwardens for Hopkin's bed and board.

In the 1674 Hearth Tax the building was listed as having 4 hearths but the first description we have of the property is in an advertisement of 1729 –
"The Crown being a large and well accustomed Inn with a very good brewing office and two convenient slaughterhouses, fitting for any country butcher to kill and dress their ware, is now to be let or sold. Enquire Mr. Charles Cutting or Charles Crow at the house aforesaid"

So as was often the case the tenant could have combined the running of an inn with another occupation, a butcher in this case. William Bunn took up the tenancy and appears at the Crown in the 1730s. He was an apothecary and brewer and was associated with both the Dukes Head and Greyhound inns in the town.

Dan Kerridge, a waggoner was calling at the Crown on Mondays in 1744 to collect packages and passengers on his regular journey to London every week, returning on Thursdays. Another advertisement appeared in 1749 and mentioned that the inn still had it's brewhouse and slaughterhouse, also stables for 40 horses.

Finally in 1755 a for sale notice appeared and we are informed that a "malt distilling office" has been added to the property, also sties for

100 hogs in an adjoining yard, granaries and a large shop fronting the street. There is now no mention of stables; maybe the pigsties had taken their place.

The impression given is of a large busy inn; the various out buildings must have extended over quite a large area. It was probably after this sale that the name was changed to the Fox And Hounds. NL

Owners

1562-1562	John Wage
1618-1619	John Wage
1624-1630	Anne Wage
1630-1671	William Wage senior
1671-1680	William Wage junior

Occupiers

1680-1690?	John King
1691-1704	Daniel Osbourne, cutler
1711-1718	Marke Wright
1718-1729	Charles Crow
1732-1734	William Longhurst
1734-1740	Thomas Bulbrook
1742-1746	Edward Martin junior
1745-1745	Widow Martin
1745-1751	Thomas Bacon
1755	William Wright

CROWN INN
Thorney Green Road/Church Road Stowupland
c.1752-present

1928

This Inn has as it's core a building that probably goes back to the 14th century. Just when it started as a hostelry is difficult to pinpoint. We do know it was a copyhold tenancy of the Manor of Thorney Hall, and that by 1752 William Aldrich was the tenant of a moiety (part) of a messuage and an orchard and a tenement lately in the occupation of Stephen Bacon. By 1763 Pelham Aldrich was the tenant and this was so until at least 1766. An advert' of 1770 informs of the sale a blacksmiths shop to be held at the pub' on Thorney Green. Another Aldrich, this time John was perhaps the owner in 1772, and it was he who sold (part?) to John Cobbold in 1805. A deed of December 11th 1811 states "John Aldrich merchant of Ipswich in the sum of £280 (£6k) paid by John Cobbold of Eye common brewer. All that undivided moiety or half part messuage or tenement, one orchard in Stowupland heretofore the estate of Edward Beverley and Dorothy his wife and also all that tenement adjoining in Stowupland heretofore the estate of Edward Bacon which said John Aldrich had under the will of his father July 2nd 1789". By 1834 brewer John Cobbold solely owned the premises.

Some landlord's feature in the newspapers of the day and it is that personal information that puts flesh on the bones of history. Viz

Benjamin Batley, Oct 1825, "on Wednesday last an inquest was held, the deceased called on Monday evening last at the house of William Baker carrier of Stowupland for two parcels, and after having put them in his cart he went into the house to pay for the carriage for them, apparently in good health. In the space of 2 minutes after sitting in the chair he was suddenly seized with a fit of apoplexy, and instantly died". 1842 Robert Burch fined 50 shillings and costs of 15/6d upon information given by William Kidney, appeal dismissed, the offence is not known. In conversation with a reporter in 1949 landlord Robert Flack said "I think this used to be a private house" speaking in his bar parlour with a low ceiling hung about with saddlery "they used to have shilling licences for selling home made beer, I think that's how it started up". Mr Flack then produced two glasses and chinked them together; they made a fine ringing sound. "Old punch glasses" he said, "for egg flip. They haven't been used for years. I've got a few old beer mugs left too. The Yanks and the South Africans bought the lot. One chap gave me 35 shillings once for a quart mug, then sat down with it in that chair, and promptly broke it, then I'm d....d if I didn't have to sell him a pint one as well".

On June 16th 1966 Alan Smethurst the "Singing Postman" a well known Norfolk celebrity visited the Crown and a video was made of his song "They're Orl Playin Dommys In The Bar". In November 1966 the building was re-thatched.

Another survivor, this establishment now serves meals and thrives in uncertain times, long may it continue. BAS

1752	Stephen Bacon occupier, a pub?
1758	Robert Herne Stowupland innholder, indemnity bond
17--	Turner before 1763
1763-1766	Christian Tricker, rent 7 pence
1768-1772	John Tricker, a John buried 1783
1806	T J B Balls cricket match
1811	William Battley occupier
1820-1825	Benjamin Batley, buried Nov 1825 age 54
1827-1874	Robert Burch, buried 1874 age 80
1874-1894	Charles Barnard, nephew of Robert Burch.

Accidental death of Barnard Dec 12th 1894, from suffocation, through falling on his face on a pillow when in a faint, age 49.

1894-1904	Mrs Mary Ann Barnard widow age 52 in 1891
1904-1929	Arthur Edward Forsdyke
1929-1964	John Robert Flack, he married Lily Makings, daughter of Thomas of the Barge
1964-1971	Hugh R Jarvis & Brenda, she was daughter of John R Flack
1971-1973	Raymond Wood
1974	Graham L & John M Wood
1975-1976	Raymond Wood
1977-1989	John C Hunting
1990	Peter R Craven
1991-1994	Steven Cooper
1995-2000	John S Collis

CROWN
Crown Street
c.1852 – current

Positioned in a prominent spot opposite the Cardinals Road railway crossing, this hostelry was probably completed in 1851 by builder Francis Betts, the beer etc was supplied by the Stonham Parva based Stonham Brewery. I suspect that the brewery purchased the pub soon after completion as they advertised for a landlord in 1855. Builder Betts had always lived in Bury Street and died there in 1868 aged just 56. In 1866, a Dorset born man 33-year-old widower Christopher Ryall bought the Crown and ran it until 1897, combining his other interests of farming & as a carrier. In 1874 he acted as surety & lost a court case over a breach of contract agreement in 1875. He had sold out to Bullard & Co of Norwich by 1898.

In August 1911 a terrible fire engulfed the building, an elderly lady was trapped upstairs & suffocated. The Crown was rebuilt almost immediately & continues to this day to quench the thirst of it's patrons. Currently it is owned by Pubmaster. BAS

Occupiers

1852 January	John Wilden beerhouse New Road.
1852-1855	Isaac Turner, a carrier
1855-1856	Henry Southgate
1856-	Ephraim Colby beerhouse Crown Road
1858-1859	Thomas Wilkins
1859-1865	Oliver Hart, wheelwright age 23 in 1861
1866-1897	Christopher Ryall & owner
1898-1925	Frederick Culley
1925-1932	Robert Lillistone
1933-1934	George Henry Chapman
1934-1945	Leonard Bird, plans to extend in 1936
1945-1963	Percy George Wright
1963-1972	Kenneth Percy Wright
1973-1975	Christopher J Potter
1976-1977	Alvine J/Christopher B/Sidney S Freeman
1978-1987	John C Wray
1988-1991	Roy E Smith
1992-1996	Jeffery P Duncan
1996-1997	Patrick Thompson
1997-	Josephine A Duncan manager for John Paton
1998-1999	Debbie Worsfield
1999-	B T Wisbey

DUKE OF WELLINGTON INN
Stowupland Road, formerly in Stowupland
c.1864 – 1975

Sorting out the two Wellingtons has been a nightmare. The main problem is the lack of rate books for Stowupland & the fact that the directories of the day could not agree on the correct name, for instance the 1865 Post Office directory lists William Sutton at the Duke of Wellington whilst all other facts show he was at the Wellington Inn! Another problem was the information given by the late Clare Gordon Robinson in his book Handlebars & Steering Wheels "It was in a small public house called the Little Wellington in the village of Stowupland that I was born on 13th of August 1904". The Cobbold brewery notebooks clearly states his father was in their pub, the 1901 census substantiate this, unless you dear reader know different!

A Mr Leeks purchased the Wellington Inn & two adjoining cottages for £480 freehold from an auction held at the Crown & Anchor Hotel in Ipswich in October 1865. The previous owners were The Stowmarket Brewery, it was leased to Phillips Brothers of Stowmarket, they continued to trade under the same name. The landlord from 1865 until 1869 was a James Leeks, presumably the same person who had purchased it. If so, then Leeks must have sold to John Cobbold almost immediately because Cobbold's note books show a rental income of £27 (£1,800) for the Wellington Inn in the January 1st account of 1866. James Leeks is shown in the 1871 census as a "retired shopkeeper" aged 33, shortly afterwards he purchased the Unicorn.

Stonemason Frederick Brett stayed just three years as landlord and was followed by James Francis of Willisham, James was involved in a court case in 1875. This pattern of landlord movements from pub to pub continued when in 1877 William Green from the White Horse arrived for a short tenure. The most colourful landlord in terms of court cases etc was Thomas Berry, aged 56 in 1881 he had previously been bankrupt in 1879 and again in 1880 when his bosses Messrs Cobbold's sued him for non payment of £20 of goods. Berry was paying £15 per quarter rent at this period. As stated in 1897, George Lewis Robinson publican and part time photographer arrived to run the pub, Robinson had been born at the Fox and Hounds Stowmarket in 1873.

By 1913 the rent had been reduced to £10 p.a.(£705) and before 1923 the pub was home to the Stowmarket Swifts F.C. The Homing Society, the Referee's Association & a slate club!. In 1931 Ernest Robert Pells started his tenure and was to become the longest serving landlord, he served until 1954 combining this with his other job at the Stowmarket Timber Works. After some 110 years of service, the end came in 1976 when Nellie Noller called "last orders" for the final time. The building now houses an alternative therapy centre. BAS

Owners
1865	Stowmarket Brewery/Phillips Brothers
1865	Mr Leeks buys for £480, including two adjoining cottages freehold.
1866	John Cobbold, rent £27-10s pa

Occupiers
1865-1869	James Leeks, to Unicorn
1869-1872	Frederick Brett, age 27 in 1871
1872-1875	James Francis, wife Margaret
1877	Samuel Pettit, interim licence
1877	William Green, interim licence
1878-1882	Thomas Berry, age 56 in 1881, also a carter

1882-1892	William Kerry jnr, & cattle dealer, age 42 in 1891
1896	Henry Soames, from Stowupland Retreat
1897	George Beaumont, to Kings Arms
1897-1908	George Lewis Robinson
1908-1913	John Ernest William Haggar
1913-1920	Percy Kerry
1920-1931	John (Jack) Webb
1931-1954	Ernest Robert Pells
1954-1969	William Victor Noller
1970-1976	Nellie E Noller

DUKES HEAD

46 Ipswich Street

[previously White Swan & Cherry Tree]

c.1660 - present

Originally a house called Pulfords [no doubt after a family who had lived there – Pulfords are recorded in the town from 17th – 19th century] which was built in 1608 on the site of an older house. It included a backhouse, slaughterhouse, shed and stable and was owned by a William Grimwood of Offton. He surrendered a "croft called Pulfords" to John Humphrey, this John Humphrey's father or grandfather; also John had been an innholder in Stowmarket in 1660 on the restoration of Charles II. Whether this previous John was at Pulfords/the White Swan is not certain. However on his death in 1666 an inventory of Humphrey's goods was taken. He is described therein as an innholder and the rooms of his house listed as comprising *"The Hall, Greate Parlor, Little Parlor, Great Parlor Chamber, Little Parlor Chamber, Hall Chamber, Buttery, Cellar, and Brew House".*

A quantity of hops was stored in the hall chamber and various brewing vessels in the brew house.

By the time John Humphreys sold to William Aldrich, an apothecary and brewer in 1706 the establishment had become the White Swan and Humphreys is described as an innholder. Aldrich passed the Inn on to his son in law Thomas Martin of Barrards Hall Whatfield, during his ownership between 1728 and 1731 the name the Cherry Tree was used.

On Thomas Martin's death in 1731 the ownership of Cherry Tree was shared between Lydia, Susan and Sarah his daughters, while his widow Mary continued to live there until her death in 1742. In 1732 Mistress Martin had a substantial amount of work done to the house. The accounts of the money expended which totalled £73:03:01 and the individual receipts from the tradesmen involved have survived with the deeds and are in the Suffolk Record Office in Ipswich.
A letter of 1741 also preserved amongst the deeds reads –

"Madm.

If you have not let the Cherry Tree I will give you thirteen pounds a year for it for four years rather than have it hired over my head. I am Madm. Your most humble servt.

Wm. Bunn
December 9. 1741"

Bunn a brewer by the time he made his will in 1750 owned the Greyhound, the Queens Head, the Angel all in Stowmarket, the Magpie in Combs Ford as well as the Maypole in Wetherden. His bid may not have been accepted, as a Francis Wright seems to have been at the inn at this time and to have stayed until 1748.

Lydia Martin married Thomas Hill of Boxford, however this marriage was short lived as Thomas died in 1744. In that year the three Martin sisters are recorded in the manorial court to have demolished a brewhouse without permission. Two years later the Inn was sold to John Rust, grocer of Stowmarket and at this time the name the Dukes Head, which remains to this day, was adopted.

Remaining in the Rust family for 3 generations the Dukes Head was purchased by brewer John Cobbold from John Edgar Rust for £615 in 1803. The Rusts and the Cobbolds were related by marriage.

For several years during the Rust ownership an Edward Simpson was tenant. He later kept the Kings Head and was twice declared bankrupt in 1795 & 1800 and was described as innholder, vintner, dealer and chapman. He died in Bath in 1805 but his descendants later established a stone masons business in Ipswich Street near the Dukes Head.

During the early 19th Century the Dukes Head acted as the posting house for the Royal Mail coaches. Post Office archive records show that in 1797 the daughter of a Mrs. Mills the then postmistress asked for permission to take over the post from her mother due to her ill health. The daughter was Elizabeth the wife of John Earthy, they lived opposite the Dukes Head and their son William later became the landlord of the inn. A War Office survey of 1916 shows that the Inn still had stabling for 30 horses.

The adjacent Dukes Head Meadow was the site of travelling fairs and circuses in the early 20th Century until the Regal Cinema was built on the site in 1935. Later a small wooden building next to the Dukes Head was used as the booking office of Combs Coaches. The coaches would pick up passengers here.

The pub continues to be a lively town centre venue. NL

Owners

Pulfords/White Swan
1640-1675   William Grimwood
1675-1675   William Grimwood junior
1675-1706   John Humphrey
1706-c.1718   William Aldrich

Cherry Tree
c.1718-1728   William Aldrich

1731-1731	Thomas Martin, son in law of William Aldrich
1742-1742	Mrs Mary Martin, widow of Thomas Martin

Dukes Head

1746-1775	John Rust, grocer
1776-1777	Thomas Rust, son of John
1798-1803	John Edgar Rust, son of Thomas
1803-	John Cobbold, brewer

Occupiers

1660-1663	John Humphrey
1666-1666	Elizabeth Humphrey
1673-1697	John Humphrey
1713-1713	Phillip Mumford
1713-1714	Samuel Purcas, grocer and brewer
1714-1715	Edmund Wainford
1715-1716	James Pulham
1716-1717	Samuel Purcas
1718-1730	Robert Aldis
1732-1734	Mrs Aldis, widow of Robert
1735-1748	Francis Wright, possibly paid poor rate
1748-1786	Edward Simpson junior
1791-1800	Isaac Hanton
1800-1803	James Hanton
1810-1823	William Earthy
1826-18??	James Ward
1830-183?	William Blondon
1834-1836	William Bird
1836-1848	John Haggar
1849-1861	John Brett
1861-1867	Robert Elllis, carpenter
1867-1868	Mrs Sarah Harvey
1868-1874	Joseph Cornelius Cooper, drowned himself, inquest
1874-1876	Mrs Matilda Cooper
1876-1883	Arnold Suttle, hay dealer
1884-1889	Mrs Caroline Elizabeth Suttle, hay/cattle dealer
1889-1892	Robert Smith, slaughterhouse licence issued for Dukes Head yard 1889, fire destroyed stables 1890

1892-1917	Alfred Game
1920-1930	Arthur Thomas Steggall, died at pub' aged 54
1930-1933	Mrs Ann Steggall
1933-1937	Edward Schnyder
1938-1951	John Ernest William Haggar
1951-1966	Kenneth George Edward Pearl, fined for sales out of hours 1962
1967-1967	P.J.C. Tricker
1967-1968	Derek Cunningham Hoult, dancing licence 1968
1969-1969	Walter A Longhurst
1970-1978	William Charles and Olive Cattermole
1979-1981	Alan C & Maureen Seal
1982-1984	Dennis W Kennedy
1985-1986	Reginald Harold W. Steed
1986-1987	Dennis W. Kennedy
1988-1991	Jonathan Hewitt
1992-1993	Michael & Zonta Melwani
1994-2000	Ronald Eric Fitch

EIGHT BELLS
Stowmarket, location unknown

1752 May 9th Ipswich Journal "John Ringe brother to Edward Simpson, wool-comber and Innkeeper at the sign of Eight Bells in Stowmarket, having died suddenly in London, and left his chest in the country, in which was his money, bills and other things, the person that has the said chest and desired to let the right owner have it (which is the abovesaid Edward Simpson wool-comber and Innkeeper at the sign of the Eight Bells) for which he shall receive a good reward". Edward Simpson Jnr was at the Dukes Head. BAS

FALCON
Stowmarket, location unknown

1711	William Good senr paid poor rate?
1714	William Good licensee
1716	Samuel Purkis (grocer/beer brewer) paid poor rate for Wm Good
1717	James Pulham paid poor rate? then in 1722 he was suppressed
1719	Samuel Purkis died (see Kings Arms)
1727	William Pettit innkeeper (1697-1772) he was the son of William senr a brewer. BAS

FLOWER DE LUZE
Combs, unknown location
Fleur de Lis "Lily flower"

Gardener Cook is known to have been at the Flower De Luze in 1619 and 1620. He had children baptized in Stowmarket between 1609 and 1618. BAS

FOUNDRY ARMS
Bury Street
1877 - after 1881

This establishment is only known from entries in the register of the town's licensed premises between 1877 and 1881. The name would suggest that it catered for the thirsty foundry workers at Suffolk Iron Works, which stood in the area behind Bury Street. BAS

FOX INN/HOTEL
27 Ipswich Street
c.1766 – 1984

'Fox' Hotel,
STOWMARKET.

Family and
Commercial.

Telephone No. 198.

Garage.
Electric Light.
Billiards.
'Bus meets all
trains.
Good Cuisine.

This grade two listed Inn occupied a prominent position in the main street of the town, just when it began life is difficult to establish. The late Harry Double wrote a piece on it "1564 the Regulator left the Fox at 11 a.m. to Bury St Edmunds, the Shannon left at 8 a.m. to connect with the London coach at the Great White Horse in Ipswich". I can find no evidence to confirm the existence of the Fox for at least the next 200 years. The inauguration of mail coaches was in 1784, the Regulator referred to is shown in Whites 1844 directory. The Rev Hollingsworth in his history of the town mentioned an Inn "The Fox Run Down" this is a misreading of Foxldown, a field name.

Dennis Chandler a local corn & coal merchant advertised it for sale in 1797 & according to the land tax bills Edward Lockwood became the owner in that year, he had at least 10 children & his tombstone informs us that he passed away in 1826 aged 85. Sarah Lockwood (almost certainly the daughter of Edward) and a person named Bridges owned the Inn from 1836 to 1849. The next known proprietor from 1850 to 1862 was John Lockwood, born in Cretingham in c1806 & a cousin of Bridges. John was widowed in 1856 when Ann his wife aged 47 passed away. In 1862 John Lockwood was made a bankrupt, the Inn was sold, at this time he married 45 year old widow Mary Ann Corner, she had been the landlady of the Pickerel for four years in nearby Stowupland. John & his new wife Mary Ann set up home at Pound Farm Bury Road next to the Bell Inn, where he farmed for the next forty years.

From 1856 to his death in 1861 John George Hart's name appears in the rate books, he was manager of the local Oakes/Bevan/Moor & Co bank. However by 1860 bank clerk Edward Bridges was the occupier, eventually becoming the owner. George Boby a successful local grocer & draper purchased the Fox in 1867, he stayed until 1878, by this time the hotel had a large complex of out-buildings, bake ovens, large carriage shed, piggeries, offices, coach houses & stables etc stretching over Church Walk to the former Vicarage grounds. The frontage of the hotel was 75 feet & the depth was some 165 feet. Here is a brief summary of the hotel when put up for auction in 1878 "large & extensive cellarage, on ground floor: mixing bar, 2 front parlours, 2 back parlours, commercial room, large market room, 2 storerooms, 2 pantries, larder, large cooking kitchen, scullery, mangle room etc, first floor: large dining room, 3 private sitting rooms, 9 bedrooms, & WC On second floor: small sitting room, 5 bedrooms, & 2 attic bedrooms". Enter Edward Bridges again, originally the occupier as discussed & owner from 1878 until his death in 1892 at the age of 61. Edward was born in Wetherden & he enrolled in the 6th Suffolk Rifle Corps at Stowmarket in February 1860, we have a short physical description of him as follows, 5 feet 7 inches tall & 29 years old, he resigned after serving 17 years.

During his tenure he initiated the Fox omnibus, this would meet every train & carry patrons to the hotel from the railway station. In March 1892 a sale of some of Edward Bridges effects was held, comprising "oil paintings, 31 prints, engravings, lithographs, silver plate, & 27 china pieces. In 1892 Edward Cooke a wine merchant from Blofield near Norwich was the purchaser, he was possibly the owner of the Stonham Brewery of Stonham Parva. In 1896 Tollemache & Co the Ipswich brewers were owners & remained so until c1917. However a curious article appeared in the Ipswich Journal of 1896, "Sale of contents puzzling, The Fox was sold to Mr Cooke upon the death of Bridges, & John Garrard became tenant, he carried on until Cooke sold to Tollemache & a change of tenancy occurred on Lady Day (March 25ᵗʰ) when Mr Le Touzel came in. Men from Hunt & Peddar (auctioneers) removed all the furniture whilst Le Touzel was in London, but his family obtained a few tables & chairs & other furniture so as to make the house habitable. It is now completely refurbished by Messrs Maple of London". Soon after Tollemache & Co became owners they put into operation large-scale extensions & alterations. A succession of owners followed from 1912 until 1929, see below. As usual many different activities took part in the hotel over the years, I have omitted those meetings, property sales, billiard tournaments etc that took place in the Fox, except to say my own wedding reception was held there in 1968. BAS

Further owners
1922   Harold Pike
1925   Coxhead & Pritchard
1929   Charles T Coxhead.

Occupiers
c.1766-1777   John Witham speculation. He had left the Angel, &
              married widow Elizabeth Wright
1775   Abutment
1783   Mrs Elizabeth Witham deceased, her goods for sale
1791-1797   Edward Lockwood paid poor rate?
1830-1861+   John Lockwood, owner/occupier, bankrupt 1862
1861-1892   Edward Bridges, excise office 1864, damaged in
              the great gun cotton explosion of 1871, occupier
              & owner from 1878, also funeral carriage proprietor

1892-1896	John Garrard
1896-1897	Giboune M Le Touzel
1897-1898	Arthur Jeffery barman
1898-1905	John Tremlett, died 1905 age 41, Samuel Clarke was "boots" in 1904
1905-1912	William Farr Stroud, accident 1906 cyclist & Fox bus
1912-1917	John Mark Richards & owner
1917-1921	John D Cable, from Windsor, bought suit at Plucks in 1919 for £1-1s
1922-	Harold Gurney
1923-	unknown, electoral roll blank
1924-	Edwin Baldwin
1925-1928	Charles T Coxhead & William C Pritchard & owners
1929-1932	Charles Thomas Coxhead
1933-	Arthur Henry Wilkinson & owner
1934-	Thomas Mottram Studd
1935-1937	George Thomas Cousens, died 1937 age 48
1937-	Mrs Gertrude Cousens
1937-1939	Arthur Edward Tunstall
1940-1949	Neil Bryne
1949-1967	Alec Douglas Bedwell, & owner
1967-1975	Brian John Ruffell & Bunty from Scarborough
1976-1977	Reginald G & Veronica K Sims, has 13 bedrooms all centrally heated
1978-	Malcolm A Little
1979-1980	Dennis N & Doris M Bennett
1981-1984	Reginald G Sims

FOX AND HOUNDS
14 Bury Street
c1756 - 1917 [previously the Crown]

F. W. Ames c.1902

By 1768 the inn was under the ownership of Pelham Aldrich and known by it's new name of the Fox And Hounds. The inn seems to have been as busy as ever as a venue for social events and as a staging point for coaches and wagons. One social event reported to have been held at the inn in 1794 was the Annual Auricular Show. A will of 1804, mentions "the sum of five pounds of lawful money....being the sum allowed and payable from the Club of Brotherly Love holden at the Fox and Hounds Stowmarket". This was probably a friendly society – members would pay a small weekly subscription and could claim help from the club's funds if they should fall ill, which at that time would mean loss of earnings.

When John Wells the tenant from 1791 to 1811 died his widow soon married Thomas Balls who was licensee at the White Lion. There often seems to have been marriages between members of Stowmarket's innkeeping community.

The Shannon coach was calling at the Fox And Hounds every morning at 7.30 according to an 1830 directory. John Brownsmith who had the inn from 1844 to 1865 had been previously listed on the 1841 census as a coachman at the inn.

By 1834 the Fox And Hounds had been added to John Cobbold's holdings in the town. It stayed with Cobbold and Co. until it's closure.

Arthur Barnard was in residence from 1885 to 1900; Arthur had come from Bury St. Edmunds and worked as a bill-poster, also collecting the market tolls and must have been a familiar figure in the town. His son Oliver founded the car trading and haulage company, O.G.Barnard and Sons. The penultimate tenant was Frederick William Ames who stayed less than two years, according to a descendent he succumbed to the temptation of having large amounts of alcohol within easy reach! Maybe wisely this was Frederick's only attempt at running a pub but his descendants became greengrocers and fishmongers in the town.

1904 saw Stephen Rushbrooke taking up the tenancy; he had previously been at the Prince Of Wales beerhouse in Ipswich Street. He was one of the longer running tenants and was still there in 1916 when the future of the Fox And Hounds was being debated, rather surprisingly this old established pub seems to have been a victim of the reduction in licensed premises which had seen many closed in the previous few years. It was referred for compensation and Cobbolds were awarded £543.14.00 and Rushbrooke £54.

The Fox And Hounds finally closed it's doors in February 1917. The building was demolished and a Co-op store was built on the site in 1925, this is at present a charity shop. NL

Owners
1768	Pelham Aldrich
1768- 1798	John Aldrich
1834-1917	Cobbolds

Occupiers

1767-1772	John Jeffrey
1791-1811	John Wells
1811-1813	Mrs Elizabeth Wells
1814-1840	John Hunt
1840-1842	Elizabeth Hunt
1842-1844	Robert Aldous Bowell
1844-1865	John Brownsmith
1865-1866	Mary Ann Brownsmith nee Hunt
1866-1870	Benjamin Bantock
1870-1873	Mary Balls, widow
1873-1876	Samuel Robinson, sued for non payment of bricks
1876-1885	Ellis Palmer Huggins, fined 20s, open out of hours 1
1885-1885	Mrs Amy Huggins
1885-1900	Arthur Barnard
1900-1902	Mrs. Margaret Barnard
1902-1904	Frederick William Ames, was in Home Defence Force, died 1937
1904-1917	Stephen Rushbrook
1917	Closed

GARDENERS ARMS
Moats Tye Upper Combs
c.1855-current

Situated in a prominent position on the corner of the road to Battisford, this picturesque building is believed to be 300-400 years old. The first recorded beerhouse owners that have been found was Mr Eliezer (hebrew "God helps") Lambert and Mr Samuel Andrews they sold the property in 1852 to William Crosse jnr. A Charlotte Crosse was the owner in 1856 until 1860 when the property was sold to Manning Prentice of the Stowmarket Brewery with Joseph Lankester a part owner. However by 1865 they advertised in the Ipswich Journal " for sale a beerhouse occupied by John Robinson, having stables and out buildings". As ever without access to the deeds the exact ownership is difficult to determine, however Alexander Clutterbuck of the Stowmarket Brewery was still involved when it was sold to Edward King in 1882.

This company evolved into Greene King by 1887. An August 1898 report states "An analysis of the water in the pond states that it is lightly polluted with vegetable organic matter and is on the whole a very good specimen of pond water" the mains supply was at last connected in 1956. On October 28th 1920 the death of Margaret Gosling was registered as having occurred in the pub, she was the wife of Thomas a previous landlord.

The landlords over the past 150 years have been many and various. Here are a few snippets.

Landlord Thomas Prior was assaulted 1876, charged with selling out of hours also in 1876, his premises broken into in 1878. George Webber a cattle dealer from Live and Let Live came in 1878 and died there in 1891 age 65. An inquest was held on the premises in 1899 when bricklayer/builder Thomas Gosling was the landlord, he also had his own business in the Ford. George Battle came from Stonham Cricketers in 1912 and stayed until his death in 1938 aged 66. Roy Cotterell (uncle of Pat' Cobbold of the Live and Let Live) was the landlord in 1939 and was to become a Dunkirk veteran, he was also at the D-Day landings. Dennis Buckle's licence was upgraded to publicans in 1962. Robert J Prior stayed until 1968 when he moved to London, but by 1971 he had returned to Suffolk to run the Buxhall Crown. Edmund J Morphew & his wife (known as Eddie & Lil) were the next occupiers; he was also a part time thatcher. In 2003 redevelopment was planned. The Gardeners Arms continues to this day and let's hope for many more years. BAS

Occupiers
1855	William Haxell upper Combs beerhouse (Gardeners?)
1863-1875	John Robinson & dealer aged 52 in 1871.
1875	Thomas Prior, interim licence refused then granted, to 1878
1878-1891	George Webber & cattle dealer
1891-1892	Margaret Webber, widow aged 43 in 1891
1892-1911	Thomas Gosling & bricklayer & builder
1912-1938	George Battle
1939	Mrs Nellie Battle
1939-1940	Roy Cotterell
1940-1946	Mrs Kathleen May Cotterell
1946-1950	Roy Cotterell
1950-1966	Dennis Buckle
1966-1968	Robert J Prior
1968-1975	Edmund J Morphew

1976-1979	Peter G & Maria E L Theobald
1980	Michael A & Maria Theobald
1981-1982	William Burch
1983-1985	Martin M Benson
1988-1987	Roy Goldwin
1988-1989	Lee Chambers
1990-1991	David J Grieves
1992	electoral roll blank
1993-1994	James F Fareden
1995-1996	Tim Reeves & Vi Stephenson
1996-1998	David E Stephens-Row
1999	Terence O Clarke
1999-2000	Nigel Burch manager, Melanie Scott landlady, but lives at Magpie
2000-2001	Richard & Jean Senior from Freston Boot
2001?-2003	Redevelopment under Barrie Pearce, meals by Malcolm Penn, B & B planned.

GEORGE
Crow Street

Scant information exists on this beerhouse, a deed of 1831 notes an abutment in Abbot Street (Crow Street) and an Ipswich Journal artical of July 1833 tells us of a theft from Mr Jannings at the George. BAS

GEORGE
Near Market Place
pre 1617 – 1713?

The precise location of the George is uncertain; it was in Ipswich Street near the Market Place, beyond that we couldn't be certain.

It's recorded life spans about 100 years and was first listed in the Mompesson account book of 1617, the landlord being Thomas Codd. The following year Francis Codd is named in the same source as the owner. Francis is also listed at Barking Cock.

After changing hands a few times it was left by William Kent, a tallow chandler of Woolpit in 1713 "with it's brewing Vessels" to William Cuthbert senior, barber.

The tenant in 1679 was John Lucas and he was paid 6 shillings in that year for billeting 2 soldiers for a fortnight.

Our main source is the account book of the overseers of the poor of the parish, the last mention of the George by name being in April 1719 when Jeremiah Bigsby paid the poor rate. However as the George is not on Devreux Edgar's licence list it appears that although still called the George it was probably William Cuthbert's barbers shop. NL

Owners
1618? -1625   Francis Codd
1653? -1664   Robert Parker, inventory 17 hogshead of beer

65

1664- 16--	Maria Parker widow of Robert
1669? -	Richard Quash
1684?- 1686	William Raymond
1686- 1689	widow Raymond
1689- 1713	William Kent late of Woolpit, tallow chandler
1713-	William Cuthbert snr, barber

Occupiers

to 1617	Thomas Codd
1618- 1625?	Thomas Griggs
1660?-1670	Nicholas Garnham
1671- 1676	Thomas Wright, cordwainer
1676- 1683	John Lucas, to Queens Head
1684?-1686	William Raymond
1686- 1689	widow Raymon(d)
1689?-	Mr Smyth
1691?	John Page
1693-1693	Francis Adams
1694-1694	Mrs Smith
1694-1697?	John Victoryn
1697?-1708	Rose Smith

GLADSTONE ARMS
Combs Ford
[previously Bold Buccleuch]
pre 1855 - present

The Gladstone Arms had an earlier name – "The Bold Buccleuch" named after a popular character in Scottish history - Walter Scott of Buccleuch, who led a raid against the English at Carlisle Castle in the reign of Elizabeth I. His namesake Sir Walter Scott made him the subject of a poem –
"He went not with the bold Buccleuch,
His banner broad to rear,
He went not 'gainst the English yew,
To lift the Scottish spear."

The name was a popular one for boats and ships and a steamer of that name traded between Hull and Yarmouth in the mid 1800s.

The name the Gladstone Arms was adopted after 1878. William Ewart Gladstone's first term as Prime Minister had begun in 1868. The new name was given during the tenancy of Robert Webb, a jobber and cattle dealer as well as a beer seller who held it from at least 1855 to 1875. We hear of him when he found himself in the petty sessions court in 1870, he was fined for allowing a horse to stray, and in 1872 he was found not guilty of selling beer to a man named Gutteridge out of hours, at the hearing it was stated that Gutteridge *"lives in a van in the yard with a prostitute"*.

His successor Frederick Robinson was also in trouble in 1878 for being drunk, and again in 1882 for opening the beerhouse after hours on a Sunday morning.

On 17th June 1879 Joseph Arch, the founder of the National Agricultural Labourers' Union and later an MP for a Norfolk Constituency addressed several hundred people in a large yard at the back of the Gladstone Arms.

Frederick Robinson had died in 1893 and his widow stayed on, running the pub until 1896. After two short tenancies the Beaumont family began their long association with the Gladstone Arms when William George Beaumont took over the licence in 1898. He had been a farmer from Badingham. His wife Sarah Maria ran a general shop from one room and on her husband's death in 1912 the licence was transferred to her. A bakery was by then being run on the premises by a son – Jesse Beaumont.

Jesse took over the licence in 1916 on his mother's death, he continued at the pub until his own death in 1938. His widow Edith Emma Beaumont continued to run it with her son Jack and his wife Eleanor [Nellie]. A Londoner, Nellie had met Jack when she was billeted at the Gladstone Arms during WWII.

Nellie's sister Marjorie also married a local boy, Ronald James and they worked at the Magpie opposite the Gladstone Arms, later moving to the Retreat in Stowupland.

Previously a beerhouse also selling wine by retail, a full licence was granted in 1949. The link with the Beaumont family that had endured over half a century ended in 1951, the Beaumont family then moved to Ipswich, Jack continued to work at ICI paints where he had been since the age of 16. When he was transferred to Slough in 1949 the family moved to Taplow.

Ind Coope and Allsopp Ltd. had taken over the ownership by 1927 from the Colchester Brewery and today it is owned by Adnams, the Southwold brewery who bought the Gladstone from Ind Coope's successors in 1992. It is the only pub owned by Adnams in the Stowmarket area. NL

Owners
1863	Bridges
1910	Colchester Brewing Co.
1927	Ind Coope & Co.
1961	Allied Breweries
1992	Adnams Plc

Occupiers
1855-1875	Robert Webb
1878-1893	Frederick Robinson
1893-1896	Ann Maria Robinson
1897-1898	George Sturgeon, 1897 fined for opening out of hours
1898-1898	Frederick Cornish
1898-1912	William George Beaumont
1912-1915	Sarah Maria Beaumont, runs a general shop in the front room
1915-1938	Jesse Beaumont
1938-1951	Edith Emma Beaumont
1951-1967	Alfred Charles Baxter
1967-1968	James S. Saunders
1968-1976	Roy Barker
1977-1989	Lesley S. & Joan P. Davis
1989-1999	Ambrose James [Jim] Grimwade
1999-	Paul & Jill Burton

GREYHOUND
Tavern Street
c.1637 – c.1799

Located in Tavern Street approximately where the old Co-op store was, the Greyhound was undoubtedly one of the premier inns of the town. An entry in manorial records suggests that a Robert Brampton owned the inn in 1669, he was granted a wine licence in 1671 but died soon after, his widow paid the poor rate in 1672 and Mistress Brampton is taxed in the hearth tax of 1674 for 10 hearths, confirming that this was a large house.

The inn was chosen in 1695 to host the High Sheriff's dinner at the time of the county assize court. The Suffolk Assizes had hastily been transferred to Stowmarket from it's usual venue – Bury St. Edmunds for reason's unknown, this was the only time it was definitely recorded as being held in the town. This choice would suggest that the inn was a large one with a room able to accommodate the many guests who would have been invited to the dinner.

At that time the inn was being run by Margaret Herne, she was the widow of James Woods who was at the inn from 1653 to 1662. She remarried to a Henry Herne and on Henry's death in 1692 continued at the inn with the help of a son by her first marriage – Charles Woods. The account signed by Charles Woods for the cost of the dinner is still preserved at the county record office in Ipswich.

Donald Black in his "Stowmarket Past and Present states that "The cellar of the Greyhound near the market place once housed prisoners when Stowmarket was an assize town. His source for this is unknown but this could relate to the assizes of 1695. A similar story is told of the Rose.

Along with several other inns in the town it is recorded in the burial register that a soldier died here in 1679 during an outbreak of disease amongst troops billeted in the town. The Ipswich Journal reports a cockfight taking place at the inn in 1751.

Henry Wilkes in an article on the history of Stowmarket printed in 1889 mentions the Greyhound; he had seen the deeds and thought it may be the oldest pub in the town. He had been told that a brewery existed there and related, "There was an ancient figure on Mr. Ray's house and shop [15 Bury Street] like a greyhound and it may at one time have been associated with the old inn". He also relates a story that "the Bosmere and Claydon volunteers were marching through the town when one volunteer took aim and shot the greyhound's head off! This must have been before 1800 as the Volunteers were disbanded in that year. For whatever reason the inn closed about 1799 although the maltings and possibly the brewery in the yard continued under the new ownership of John Cobbold.

In 1850 the property is described as previously an inn, formerly used as a brewhouse and maltings. Now partly occupied by John Footman, partly occupied by Wm. Hewitt & iron foundry, manufacturer of agricultural implements by James Woods. Footman's was a factory manufacturing corsets. NL

Owners
1637	James Barnewell of Dublin, mortgages to Richard Kyan
1669	Robert Brampton
16??-1683	Richard Keyan
1683-1696	Mary Keyan
1702-1711	Richard Keyan, gardener in St. Helens parish Ipswich
1714-1714	Thomas Read, blacksmith
1714-171?	Daniel Lock
1718-17??	Hunlocke?
1732-1735	Edward Lynch of Ipswich and Daniel Locke, cheeseman of Ipswich
1735-1750	William Bunn
1750-1762	William Aldrich, son in law of William Bunn
1762-1768	Pelham Aldrich, son of William Aldrich

1768-17??	William Aldrich of Blakenham
17??-1797	John Aldrich
1797-1797	John Aldrich inherits from father John Aldrich, he died 4 days later
1797-1810	John Aldrich, mortgaged to John Cobbold 1805
1799	Closed as an inn
1810	Property sold to John Cobbold

Occupiers

1653-1662	James Woods?
1662-1674	Margaret Woods, widow of James then married Henry Herne
1674-1692	Henry Herne
1692-1700	Margaret Herne
1700-1715	Charles Woods, son of James & Margaret Woods
1715-1750	William Bunn
1750-1763	Henry Fincham
1763-1769	Joseph Lamb from Wisbech
1769-1770	Samuel Sexton
1770-17??	Elisha Wallinger, late waiter Cross Tavern Ipswich, then to Coddenham Crown, drowned himself 1780
1775 - 1783	James Payne [?]
1783 - 17??	Simon Jackaman
c1799	closed

HAT AND FEATHER
Ipswich Street
pre 1674 – c.1772

It has been difficult to pinpoint the exact site of this tavern, fortunately there is a deed that gives us a good indication of it's position in relationship to the first congregational church, it seems therefore to have been opposite what is now Hicks Electrical Store. An Ipswich Journal advert' proudly states "situate in the most public & best street in town for business"

John North seems to have paid the poor rate from at least 1674, his first marriage was to Barbarie (sic) Baxter in Stowmarket, however this was the era of the plague & at least three of his former wives are in the town's churchyard. He himself died in 1720 at the age of 82; at one time a tombstone recorded his passing. John produced five children, the last, a daughter named Margaret was born in 1683; she married inn-holder John Crane at Combs in 1710. Being the main beneficiary of her father's will (made 1717) Margaret & husband John Crane moved into the pub' in 1720, John passing away in 1742. Mary Crane the daughter of John and Margaret ran the business until 1744.

Thomas Pearl, born c1709 seems to be the next owner, he moved to the Hat & Feather in 1744, he eventually sold out to William Aldrich in 1752 & Thomas immediately purchased the Kings Head.

After he purchased the Hat & Feather Aldrich probably owned it until his death in 1767. His story is long & complicated, in a nutshell he was almost certainly a medic as was his father. He owned at least 6 pubs in the area and died in 1767 leaving his properties to son Pelham, unfortunately Pelham died after just one year, & in turn by his will left everything to his son John. Whether the Hat & Feather was included in the bequests is unknown, but it seems likely.

Occupier William Mills advertised in 1755 that the Hat & Feather was to be let, " that ancient & well-accustomed public house & tavern situated in the most public street, consisting of 5 lower rooms,

4 chambers, 2 large cellars, a wine vault & 3 stables with a handsome garden". William probably moved to the Bull. The last known mention of this tavern was in 1772 when a horse sale was advertised to be held there. BAS

<u>Additional</u>

1666	Burial Barberye (sic), wife John North
1668	Burial Mary, daughter John North
1669	Burial Ann, wife John North
1678/9	John Odde, a souldier (sic) under Capt. Strider died at Hat & Feather
1678	Burial Joan, wife John North
1680	Burial at John North's Hat & Feather, John Cape a tanner & stranger
1724	John Crane at Feathers, Sun Insurance
1762-1781?	John Hunt, occupier & draper
1764	A James Hunt paid poor rate.

HOP POLE TAVERN
Timber Green Stowupland
c.1856-1925

After closure

Hop production in England & Wales in 1852 was at an all time high, with 46,157 acres producing 51,102,494 lbs. The area in & around Stowmarket was an early site for hop production, indeed the hop plant can still be found in the hedges in the town so the name for this beerhouse comes as no surprise. The hop plant grows at a phenomenal rate & has to be supported on a framework of wires & poles. In 1856 Norwich brewers Steward and Patterson ran an advert' in the Suffolk Chronicle that the Hop Pole was to be let. Whether they owned the premises is unclear, however in 1877 Lankester & Wells occupied the building and used it as their bonded warehouse, Alexander Clutterbuck who traded as the Stowmarket Brewery supervised the changeover. The Hop Pole was situated at the far right of the warehouse, and known locally as the "Poor Man's Hotel" due to the large number of workmen that stayed there during the week and returned home to the nearby villages at weekends. The central part of the warehouse had an archway, with the most unusual situation of a railway siding going through the building and terminating at the malthouses across the river on the Stowmarket side.

Eustace Frederick Lankester the third generation of grocers/wine merchants was born in Stowmarket in 1835, by 1881 he was living at Springfields Stricklands Road, the other partner Robert Wells was born in Aldbourne Wiltshire in c1813 and lived at Hillside Ipswich Road Stowmarket from c1875 to c1892.

Robert Thurston was landlord from 1864 to his death in 1875 aged 49, he was a most colourful character being charged with assault in 1864, case dismissed, fined £1-5s for keeping dogs without a licence in 1868, and drunk at Needham Market fined 17 shillings in 1870 (unfit landlord). Clothing was stolen from the premises in 1870, in another case of 1875 a policeman was assaulted, the landlord had called the police. The next occupier was Grayston Coleman who worked at the Suffolk Iron Works Bury Street, he left the pub' in c1880 and the next we hear of him was in Newmarket in October 1910, when the ex-jobbing gardener committed suicide aged about 60. By 1894 James Cobbold was the tenant and he is mentioned several times in the newspapers, apparently he did early morning work and was of an advanced age. In December 1909 he was carting goods for the New Explosives Co when he broke both legs leaving him in a critical condition, he was buried on 20th December 1909 at the age of 72 years.

Falling trade was no doubt one of the reasons that brought about the end in 1925, the ex public house was divided and two families occupied the houses for many more years, the whole complex was demolished in April 1972. BAS

Owners

1856	Steward & Patterson
1858	Mr William Downs
c1875	Lankester & Wells
1897	Robert Wells of Bournemouth
c1904	Lankester Wells & Bartlett Ltd
1919-1917	Mr Eugene Wells of Buxhall
1919	Green, King

Occupiers
1855	Elijah Luskie at Hop Pole farm
1858-1861	William Powell, age 41 in 1861
1862	H J Bridges
1863-1864	David Greengrass, foreman coal deliverer, charged with embezzlement
1864-1875	Robert Thurston, died August 1875 age 49
1876-1879+	Grayston Coleman
1881-1883	William Foster age 50 in 1881, charged with assault on wife
1883-1892+	Arthur James Cornell, insurance agent, fire brigade foreman, died 1895
1894-1909	James Cobbold, wife Rebecca, from White Horse, accident, died 1909 age 72
1910-1918	Herbert Parr (grandson of above James) buried November 1918 age 42
1919-1925	Arthur Lewis Hubbard
1926	beerhouse with no occupier, owned by East Suffolk CC

HORSE AND GROOM
[known as Norwich Ale Stores after c1884]
3 Station Road
c.1863 – 1911

The Horse And Groom was trading as a beerhouse by 1866 and possibly from 1863. Variously described as a beerhouse, an eating house and coffee rooms it was situated next to an existing inn – the Queens Head.

The building is two bays of a three bay early 15th century timber framed house. The original appearance would have been similar to the existing building on the other side of the adjoining Oriental Fountain Restaurant.

For most of it's life as a beerhouse it was owned by members of the Hatton family of Great Finborough who also owned the adjoining house and other property in the town, but was leased to various breweries. Firstly the Stonham Brewery seems to have leased the premises at the beginning of this period but from 1875 to 1880 William Golland Ranson of the brewery in Violet Hill leased the house.

The owner was George Hatton from 1863 to 1878 and after his

death in that year by his executors and then by 2 further members of the family. There were a string of short tenancies for the first 20 years of it's existence but after the departure of John Thurston to the neighbouring Queens Head in 1883 Frederick Barnard began his tenure of 26 years, also carrying on his occupation of fishmonger, already with experience of selling beer at the Staff Of Life.

The final years of this beerhouse saw Frederick Barnard moving to the Bakers Arms in Violet Hill Road and handing over to the last landlord – John James Timworth who remained until closure in 1911 at which time the beerhouse was leased to Morgans Norwich Brewery.

Soon afterwards the Dykes family who already ran the Gordon Temperance Hotel next door established a bicycle shop here. Until recently the building was a shop trading as Babytime. NL

Owners
1863-1878   George Hatton
1878-1880   George Hatton executors
1880-1895   William Hatton and his executors
1896-1911   J & G. Gudgeon/late George Hatton's beneficiaries

Occupiers
1863-1864   Hansord J. Bridges, manager for Benjamin Dawson
             [Stonham Brewery]
1866-1871   Jacob Presland & eating house
1871-1875   Samuel McFeters, tailor, 1875 case, dismissed for
             staying open too long
1876-1876   Amos Harding
1877-1879   Robert Durrant, 1878 was assaulted, 1878
             complaint against
1879-1880   George Flowers
1880-1881   John Rivers of Framlingham
1881-1883   John Thurston & coach wheeler
1909-1909   Frederick Barnard. 1891 butcher Leonard Pattle
             fined for throwing a bucket of hot water over
             a retriever owned by Fred & Mary Barnard,
             fishmongers.
1909-1911   John James Timworth

KINGS ARMS
Stowmarket, location unknown
c.1617 -

The first mention of an inn using the sign of the Kings Arms in Stowmarket is in the account books of Giles Mompesson.

Mompesson had obtained a patent, which authorised him to licence inns throughout the country and receive the licence money. He was impeached in 1621 for abuse of his patent, however his account books survive and these are a valuable resource as they give the names of both the inn and the innholder, one copy of the account book is kept at Buckingham County Record Office. Between 1617 & 1620 a John Reade is named as the innholder of the Kings Arms.

This is confirmed by the entry in the Lent Recognizances of 1619 [which bound victuallers and innkeepers not to sell meat during lent and at other times when it was forbidden], which gives the names John and Robert Reade as occupiers. A John Reade was buried in Stowmarket in 1630.

There is no further record of a Kings Arms in the town until 1669 so it is doubtful if these two establishments were the same, however as the use of signs representing the monarch would have been forbidden during the period of the commonwealth this inn may have gone under a different name, returning to the Kings Arms on the restoration in 1660. NL

Occupier
1617-1620   John Reade

KINGS ARMS
Ipswich Street
c. 1660 - 1847

c.1872 after closure

Although this could be the same inn as that described in the previous chapter it will be dealt with separately here.

Hollingsworth in his History of Stowmarket states that the Inn dates from 1660 and was an "old sign made new". This may mean that the sign used during the Commonwealth, when the depiction of the monarch would have been forbidden and the inn may have gone under a different sign had been repainted on the restoration in 1660. Hollingsworth had access to records, which have now been lost, and this may either have been based on these records or have been speculation [as a fair share of his history was]. A more definite date fact is that in 1676 an entry in the manorial records stated that William Turner asked permission of the court to erect a sign post on waste next to his house "and his house is now called the Kings Arms in Ipswich Street" together with the fact that William Turner was granted a wine licence in 1677 seems to give a fairly reliable date for the establishment of the inn. Either way Hillingsworth names a J. Wright as the innholder when in 1679 we read in the burial register of the parish that Henry Hayes "a young lad came with the soldiers" died at the Kings Arms, this was the last victim of the smallpox outbreak that swept through the soldiers billeted at the towns inns at that time.

In 1719 the Kings Arms was owned by William Goodwin, a brass founder and his wife Jane nee Wright, it is described in the deeds as "now divided into tenements, lately new built (or part thereof)." Comprising "one cellar, one shoppe over the cellar, one chamber and garrett over the same, two low roomes behind the said shoppe with three chambers and two garretts over them, the shoppe called the foundering shoppe adjoining the malt house there near with two chambers and two garretts over them and stable abutting upon the camping ground towards the south and the west and a hay chamber over it. One garden lately paled out with use of well and pump ". This shows that William Goodwin or his son William also a brass founder had a foundry on the premises, there is no mention that it was being used as an inn at that time, but the presence of a malt house and stables indicates that it was.

1775 saw the inn in the ownership of Mr Leonard Munnings, he was mentioned in the autobiography of William Godwin, the writer and father of Mary Shelley, who briefly ministered at the nearby Independent Meeting House in 1781-82 as follows "The only pleasant acquaintance I had here was Mrs. Alice Munnings and her unfortunate son Leonard, a Captain of the Suffolk militia, and a lively, well bred and intelligent man" Why Leonard was unfortunate is not known!

The property passed to Leonard's son, Shadrach Munnings, a merchant of Narborough in Norfolk. By 1792 Shadrach Munnings is described as "now in Brussels", possibly on business, or maybe he was forced to live there due to debt. Debtors and bankrupts would often go to live on the continent due to the cheaper cost of living there.

At this time the Kings Arms came into the hands of John Boby of Stowupland, who in his will, made and proved in 1817 left the property to his heirs Robert & Charles Boby. A plan of this date drawn on one of the deeds shows the inn and adjoining buildings and is the only illustration we have of the inn.

The year after, the Kings Arms came into the hands of John Cobbold the Ipswich brewer and Robert Lockwood the occupier had been given notice to quit.

At this time the inn was being used as a staging post for coaches and the Ipswich Journal tells us that the coach from Bury called every morning at 4.

Between 1836 and 1847 Henry Cross [brother of J. G. Crosse, the Norwich surgeon] ran the inn, also being described as a farmer and auctioneer. 1847 saw the closure of the Kings Arms as an inn when it was sold to Thomas Sheldrake, for use as a shop. In January John Medland Clark who two years previously had designed the Ipswich Customs House was advertising for tenders to carry out the alterations to the building in readiness for it's new role.
The closure of the inn may not be unconnected with the arrival of the railway from London in late 1846, this saw a sharp decline in the coaching trade. The closure was probably made for good business reasons by John Cobbold, who was also chairman of the Eastern Railway Company and owned the Kings Head the premier inn of the town just a few yards away.
The building that had been the Kings Arms later became William Turners drapers shop, this continued throughout the first part of the 1900s until it was demolished in 1970. The Argos store now occupies the site. NL

Owners
1669-1696	John Wright
1717-1747	William Goodwin senior and junior
1747-1748	John Burkitt senior and junior
1748-1775	Leonard Munnings
1775-1792	Shadrack Munnings
1792-1817	John Boby
1817-1818	Robert and Charles Boby
1818-1818	Cobbold and Aldridge
1818-1846	Thomas Sheldrake

Occupiers

1673-1678	Thomas Offwood, then at the White Lion
1682-1684	Christopher Lee, then at Ipswich Bull?
1684-1689	Thomas Hayward, glover
16??-16??	John Pooley
1696-16??	William Pettitt
1714-1733	John Bowell, 1719 lately rebuilt (or part thereof) 1720 horse stolen
1733-1740	Samuel Colson
1740-1778	James Hunt
1778-17??	Duffield Offord
1780-1783	John Arthy/Earthy, 1783 Wm Smith stole from him
1785-178?	Richard Robinson
1788-1795	John Philby
1798-1818	Robert Lockwood, 1805 lost money
1818-1825	Thomas Dauncy/Dansie
1825-1832	Mary Dansie [widow of Thomas]
1832-1847	Henry Cross [married Mary Dansie]

KINGS ARMS
Station Approach
c.1850 - 1958

1950

Opened soon after the closure of an inn of the same name in Ipswich Street, this establishment was started by John Cobbold to take advantage of the trade generated by the newly arrived railway from Ipswich and London. It was opened to respond to the Railway Tavern opposite, this had been started at much the same time by the Tollemache Brewery, then a rival brewery. It is remarkable for the fact that for nearly it's whole life as a pub, just over a hundred years, just two families ran it.

The first mention is in a directory of 1850 when a Charles Edmonds was landlord. He however was soon replaced by Hunter Bewley who also continued his trade of tailoring here and remained until his

Beaumont family with the two sisters Mabel & Jessie, with Southgate at rear

85

early death in 1863 aged 48.

On his death Hunter's widow Eliza took on the running of the pub helped by her son also Hunter who returned from London where he had been following his father's trade as a tailor. Hunter was also a member of Stowmarket Rifle Volunteer Corp; he however also died young in 1875 aged just 35.

Eliza Bewley was still running the Kings Arms at the age of 72 in 1891 with the help of another son George, a niece and one servant girl. Eliza died that year and George took on the licence for a few years, but by 1896 the long association of the Bewley family with the Kings Arms was over.

The name by which the Kings Arms came to be unofficially known – "The Two Sisters" derived from Mabel Harriett and Jessie Hilda Beaumont. Their parents Arthur and Charlotte Beaumont had the pub from 1897 until 1908, the two girls learnt their trade working behind the bar. On their mother Charlotte's death Mabel and Jessie ran the pub with Mabel's husband Frank Southgate now the licence holder. Frank had formerly worked as an examiner on the railway.

On their retirement in 1948 Frank and Mabel Southgate were interviewed for the local newspaper along with Jessie Hilda now married to Mr Taylor. The span of 51 years that the family had been associated with the pub was remarkable. They remembered the heyday of the Kings Arms when the workers at the Explosives Factory would buy beer there in gallon bottles running up as much as £5 on credit. Mrs Taylor was proud of the fact that they ran an orderly house, claiming there had never been cause to call the police. Frank Southgate could claim the longest continuous licence in the town at 41 years.

Harold John Woolner and his wife succeeded them; he had been an officer in the Suffolk Police Force. The Woolners were here for 10 years. The next landlord, Kenneth Walter Girling however was to be the last, closure came on 6th May 1958.

The building has since had a variety of uses including a stationary retailer and a tanning parlour. NL

Owners
Pre 1850-1958 Cobbold & Co.

Occupiers

18??-1850	Charles Edmonds
1851-1863	Hunter Bewley senior
1863-1875	Hunter Bewley junior, 1866 joined Sffk Rifle Vol Corps, 5ft 8" age 27
1875-1891	Eliza Bewley, 1878 fined serving out of hours, 1887 robbed, money recovered,
1892-1895	George Bewley, engineer
1896-1897	James Jordan, railway porter
1897-1903	Arthur Beaumont
1903-1908	Charlotte Beaumont
1908-1948	Frank Southgate
1948-1958	Harold John Woolner
1958-1958	Kenneth Walter Girling
	Closed 6th May 1958

KINGS HEAD
14 Ipswich Street
1617? - 1963

c.1905

The Kings Head is surely one of the most sorely missed of Stowmarket's old inns. It's demolition in the 1960s was the harbinger of the wholesale demolition of most of that side of Ipswich Street in the following few years. Many old buildings were torn down only to be replaced by functional but anonymous brick units, ironically themselves now due to be swept away under a plan to reconstruct the north side of the street. Fortunately however the beautiful Jacobean staircase was saved, it was installed into Moat Farm Little Finborough (Stowmarket Mercury Jan 1964). Another snippit comes from the Shell Guide of 1960 "contains Stuart moulded plaster in the billiard room".

There was also a boxing booth within the main complex in circa 1903. It is however not easy to establish the early history of this inn. The first mention of an Inn named the Kings Head is in the Mompesson Accounts of 1617 when Thomas Mason is listed at the Inn, he was still there in the accounts of 1620. There is then a long gap in our knowledge after that date and whether this Kings Head was the building in Ipswich Street is not known for certain. Hollingsworth was of the opinion the inn had existed since 1660, reasoning that an inn with that name would not have been permitted during the period of the Commonwealth. Could the early Kings Head have changed it's name during this period, reverting to the old name on the restoration of the monarchy?.

The name is recorded in the overseers poor rate accounts from 1677 to 1681. We also know the name of the first recorded owner, this has recentlly been disovered in the court books of the manor. The Kings Head is not listed in Edgar Devereux's list of licences for the town in his notebook of 1714, suggesting that it wasn't trading then. In 1752 John Inman blacksmith sold the messuage "formerly called the Kings Head" to Thomas Pearl and a plan shows this to be 14 Ipswich Street. From around this time the inn existed continuously until it's closure in 1963. As with many of the inns in the town the Kings Head had an adjacent malting and brewhouse.

In 1792 the Bury and Norwich Post mentions a meeting of Protestant Dissenters indicating that the inn would have had a large room for such meetings. In 1805 Samuel Waters previously of the Swan at Woolpit took over the running of the inn, he was to stay for over twenty years. Post chaises and horses were available at the inn and Richard Bartrum of Ipswich ran this side of the business. A set meal known as an "ordinary" was served on market days. The Inn continued to be one of the main venues for auctions, meetings and performances, as in 1808 when John Crosse in his diary notes that "The young ladies went to a Conjuring performance at the Kings Head".

When the old White Hart, which had been situated a short distance along Ipswich Street in the Market Place closed in 1808 Samuel Waters was not slow in advertising that "In consequence of the White Hart being discontinued Samuel Waters is fitting up his house in a commodious manner".

The ownership of the inn at this time seems to have been divided amongst a number of people, an auction of shares in 1825 shows that William Stutter, gentleman of Stowmarket had a three elevenths share in the business. Samuel Waters finally departed in 1827 when a notice appears in the Ipswich Journal. "S. Waters returns his most grateful acknowledgements to his friends and public in general for support during 21 years, he has declined business in favour of N. T. Codd." In the same edition of the paper we read, "N. Thurston Codd from the Angel Inn Bramford takes the Kings Head. Well aired beds, neat post chaises with able horses & careful drivers." There was much competition between Inns at this time for coaching business, in 1830 the coach between Ipswich and Bury called at the Kings Head every day at 11.30. On the death of Samuel Waters, who had retained a financial interest in the inn, in 1834 the following appeared in the Ipswich Journal. "Old established posting inn to be sold by auction, on 28th Aug. by direction of executors of Mr. Samuel Waters deceased. Three 11th parts of the above Inn in occupation of N. T. Codd, lease expires 11th Oct 1839, yearly rent £110. Also beneficial interest in lease granted to Sam. Waters by Mr. Wm Stutter also piece of freehold ground at back of Inn yard 105 ft by 38 1/2 ft. with stables & other buildings, executors J.G. Hart & Thomas Sheldrake. Mr. Ransom, solicitor" John Cobbold, the Ipswich Brewer who already owned several Inns and public houses in the town must have purchased an interest in the inn at this time as in the rate book of 1836 he and other unnamed share holders are shown as owners, and a few years later he is the sole owner. Nathaniel Thurston Codd is last mentioned as landlord in 1839. He was landlord at the Rose in Stowmarket to 1855 and died in 1867. Henry Shuckforth Downing, who was also an auctioneer came in 1843.

An omnibus service ran from the inn to meet the trains at Colchester Station until the Railway arrived at Stowmarket in 1847. This event had a great effect on the inns of the town that had previously depended for much of their trade on the coaches that passed through the town, and from this time we see more Inns and public houses being opened in Station Road to take advantage of the custom that the railway brought. John Cobbold closed the Kings Arms at this time, which he also owned and which stood only a few yards away from the Kings Head. Some damage was done in 1871 due to the Explosion at the Gun Cotton Factory, which shook the town damaging many buildings.

The coming of the motor car revived the fortunes of the inns, in the centre of the town and the Kings Head remained a going concern, and may well have still been a cherished part of Stowmarket's heritage today if it had not been swept away much to the subsequent regret of many in the town. NL

Owners

16??-1678	John Thompson
1678-1???	Joseph Thompson, aged 20 years or thereabouts & "biggest" son of John
17??-1752	John Inman, blacksmith, "former Kings Head"
1752-1781	Thomas Pearl
1781-1784	Sarah Pearl
1784-1791	William Pearle son of Sarah Pearl, bankrupt 1791
1791-1794	Edward Simpson, nephew of Sarah Pearl, lets post horses 1794
1794-1795	Edward Simpson, son of Edward, bankrupt 1795 died at Bath 1805
1798-1802	William Jackson, son in law of Thomas Pearl formerly of Barton Mills Bull
1805-1827	Samuel Waters, from Woolpit Swan
1834-1840	John Cobbold, part owner
1832-1846	James Hacon, part owner
1840-1846	William Cumby of Chedgrave Norfolk, part owner
1833-1846	Robert Beckham of Norwich, part owner
1859-	Cobbold and son

Occupiers

It is presumed that some of the above owners also occupied and ran the inn.

1677-1681	Robert Rush
1795-179?	John Dyball, from Greyhound Chelmsford
1827-1841	Nathaniel Thurston Codd, from Bramford Angel, later to the Rose
1841	Mary Codd
1842-1843	Thomas Bailey
1843-1862	Henry Shuckforth Downing, auctioneer, then Bath House, Felixstowe
1862-1876	Joseph Bull Emery, from White Hart Wisbech, his dog Blondin attacked him 1865

1876-1883	Henry Knights, late editor/publisher of Ipswich Journal
1883-1884	Alexander Dalgety late Peckham goldsmith & John Willoughby
1885-1897	Alexander Dalgety
1887	Frank Harold Johnson, drunk, refused licence
1887-1889	David Canham, sued another landlord in 1889, bankrupt, twice fined for assault
1890-1899	Thomas George Tweed, overturned his sleigh while coming home in 1897
1899-1903	Charles Henry Whittell
1903-1908	Edward James Houghton
1908-1917	James Clement Gray, bankrupt, in Sffk Yeomanry & medically discharged
1917-1934	Gladys Constance Stanley Gray, owner & wife of James
1935-1941	James William Gray, educated Eastward Ho!, air raid damage 1941
1941-1946	Constance Julia Gray
1946-1963	James William Gray again, presumably had been in world war two, died 1963.
1963	Mrs Gladys Quirke manageress for P K Williams Bankers, ceased trading March 1963.

LITTLE WELLINGTON
12 Stowupland Road, formerly in Stowupland
c.1850 - current

1914

Sir Arthur Wellesley the first Duke of Wellington was prime minister in 1830, in his act of that year he freed beer from the licensing laws to discourage people from drinking gin which was cheap, in an effort to reduce drunkenness. However within one year there were 30,000 new beerhouses, this was possibly not the intended effect of the legislation. The earliest date found for an occupier of this beerhouse is the census of 1851 when my ancestor Frederick Webb was in residence. Frederick was born in town in 1793 & during his long life was also a maltster and corn porter; he passed away at the age of 91. His son Francis may well have followed him in the beerhouse.

One of the longest serving Stowmarket landlords was William Sutton. He was born in Combs in c1816 & in addition to running the pub (from 1854 to 1887) he had several other enterprises, being a farmer, steam engine proprietor and cattle dealer. His wife Elizabeth died in December 1880 aged just 58, and he was then assisted by his 23-year-old grandson Frederick who unfortunately died some two years later. William remarried a Caroline, and after he passed away in 1893 he was buried with his first wife Elizabeth. The house to the left of the Little Wellington (now 14 Stowupland Road) is named Sutton

House and he and his son William had lived there at various times. By 1912 Arthur Thomas Steggall was the landlord, in 1914 the pub were winners of the Thurlow Challenge Shield & the Goldsmith Challenge Cup bowls matches, the Bowls Club had been formed in 1902. Arthur served in the Great War fortunately returning home safe in 1919; his wife Annie ran the business during his enforced absence. The couple soon moved to the Dukes Head in town. By 1919 Charles Forsdyke took up residence and stayed until his death 13 years later. Other landlords came & went until in 1962 Cecil Jock Frederick Rivers took over, known as "Buzzer" he was 56 years old and after his demob' from the Royal Corps of Signals in 1945 he worked for Eastern Electricity. His wife Christine ran the pub during the day and Buzzer took over in the evenings. By 1974 the Little Wellington had a manager, Ronald Thomas Morris was 35 years old and had previously served in the RAF at nearby Wattisham.

After more than 150 years the Little Wellington continues and long may it do so. BAS

Owners
| 1854 - 1855 | Stevens & Co |
| | Green, King |

Occupiers
1851	Frederick Webb
1853	Francis Webb?
1854-1887	William Sutton, age 43 in 1861
1887-1897	Joseph Suttle, foreman at chemical works, died age 62 in 1897
1900-1902	Frederick William Francis, age 36 in 1901
1904-1909	Frederick Wilden
1909-1910	Ernest George Hughes, from Ipswich
1911-1912	William Francis Ignatius Simpson, born c1884 founder of Simpsons Toy Shop Bury Street
1912-1916	Arthur Thomas Steggall, court case 1915
1917	Mrs Annie Steggall
1919	Arthur Thomas Steggall, to Dukes Head by May 1920
1919	Hubbard
1919-1933	Charles Forsdyke, died 1933

1933-1957	Mrs Amelia (Millie) Forsdyke, died 1957, son Edward (Ted) helped out
1957-1962	Robert George Bishop, publicans licence Feb 2nd 1958.
1962-1973	Cecil Jock Frederick Rivers
1973-1974?	Ronald Thomas Morris
1974-1980	Alan A & Dorothy P Hollocks
1981-1992	Roger F Smith
1993-2000	Lesley G Gifford
2002-	Trevor & Karina Theobald, from the Royal Oak.

LIVE AND LET LIVE
Hadleigh Road (now Park Road) Combs
c.1865 – 1989

1987 Hurricane damage

Situated at Trickers Green Combs, this beerhouse seems to have been built by a Mr Roper for his two sons using clay from the nearby pond, this was a common building material at the time. A John Roper was a shopkeeper c1844-1855, and the 1861 census shows 74 year John as a householder and his wife Sarah Ann aged 39, with sons Frederick aged 15 and James aged 13 making up the family. The building was eventually bricked over, maybe some 70 years later. Beer was originally brewed on the premises, but by at least 1910 the business was owned by Green, King. In 1957 a wine licence was granted followed by a publicans licence in 1960. The pub suffered some damage in the "hurricane" of 1987, most notably the sign. After closure in November 1989 it was converted to a home and is today (2002) named Baytree House, the present owners were then in the process of further extensions.

On October 9th 1940 Combs Home Guard member Harry Rowe, who lived in nearby Jacks Lane received a warning from the local HQ of an impending invasion. He donned his denims, got his rifle and proceeded on his bicycle to Combs Command Post, on his way he called at the Magpie Inn and the Live and Let Live, he was well aware that there was no place like pubs for spreading the news! Two more stories regarding Harry have been related to me, asked what he would do if the Germans came he said " If they come I'll strike 'em on the skull with me walking stick". On another occasion during the "black out" he wanted to put some rubbish in the bin outside in the backyard of the pub, other people said they would do it for him but he insisted, there followed an almighty splash and there was Harry in the pond! One more wartime story, two men called at the Live & asked the way to Wattisham Aerodrome, they were told "up the road turn left, turn right & turn left again" to which one of the men said "you must be daft" the regular of the pub replied "I might be daft but I 'int lost".

1956

One or two previous landlords had brushes with the law, in 1882 Frederick Punchard had his watch stolen, and in a court case of January 1887 Combs labourer Albert Hearn was charged with stealing it. But far the most colourful character was landlord George Ernest Elvin Faiers, who in 1948 was committed to the assizes for unlawful wounding and sentenced to 6 months imprisonment. Faiers had found his wife Eva in a compromising position with another man and stabbed her, however they did eventually patch things up. One well known personality that visited landlord John Cobbold and his wife Pat' was the late DJ John Peel, in 1985/6 he recorded an edition of "Down Your Way" at the pub, this was a popular Radio 4 programme. John Peel lived at Great Finborough, just a short distance away through Jacks Lane. BAS

Occupiers

1869	William Roper Combs beerhouse
1870-1878	George Webber age 45 in 1871
1878-1879	Frederick Robinson, Trickers Green
1881-1882	Frederick Punchard
1883-1922?	Thomas Webb & bootmaker, age 42 years in 1901
1922-1933	Charles Edward Wilden, he also ran Stowmarket Rose & Crown
1934-1948	George Ernest Elvin Faiers
1948	temporary licence F W Woodroffe, manager of Royal Oak
1948-1952	John Lyles Carter, farm & tannery worker, & wife Nora from Thurston Fox & Hounds
1952-1984	John Lionel Cobbold, keen footballer, 34 years at tannery, a supervisor in finishing dept'
1984-1989	Patsy (Pat) Emily Cobbold, daughter of John Carter & widow of John Cobbold

MAGPIE/PIE
Combs Ford
Pre 1619 – current

Situated in an excellent spot in Combs Ford square this late? 16th century building competed with many local beerhouses and pubs, namely the Volunteers, Bakers Arms and the Gladstone Arms all within a few yards of it's doors.

The Darkin family are the first known owners/landlords, starting with Anthony in about 1619 until his death in 1667. Anthony left the property to his son Mark; he ran the business until his own demise in 1691 when unusually he leased the Pye to his son Anthony. Mr Cooke of Combs Pye is mentioned in a mortgage from George Morden in 1660. Richard Keyan is the next known owner; he was there sometime before 1709. A Thomas Reed followed him in 1709. A Thomas Brook & Elizabeth his wife were owners/occupiers around this period. Argor Catchpole (see the Angel) mortgaged the Pye to Eleanor Harvey in November 1717. By 1719 it was mortgaged again, this time to Mary Jacob (the married daughter of the aforesaid Eleanor

Harvey)' & Eleanor her other daughter to a Mr Debnam (see Angel), another owner/occupier before 1721 was a Thomas Peck. 1726 seems to be the last time it was referred to as the Pie.

In 1734 it was sold by Mrs Judith Catchpole (widow of Argor) & Thomas Catchpole (grandson of Argor) to William Bunn. The brewing empire of Bunn in just the Stowmarket/Combs area was significant, he owned the Angel, Cherry Tree (Dukes Head) Greyhound, Queens Head, Cock & Pye & the Crown. Bunn made his will on December 21st 1750 leaving all his property to his son in law William Aldrich. The Pie then went through the various members of the Aldrich family until 1805 when John Cobbold bought it.

In 1808 the coach from Bury St Edmunds to Ipswich overturned near Stowmarket, the only passenger injured was a prisoner condemned to be transported, he sustained a fractured leg & was kept at the Magpie. The doctor of the town Thomas Bayley attended to him until he was fit to resume his journey. The national brewing firm Pubmaster acquired the property in 2000. BAS

Occupiers

1619-	Anthony Darkin, in town 1641 & buried 1667
1660-	John Hayward?
1667-1691	Mark Darkin, son of Anthony
1691-	Anthony Darkin, son of Mark
unkn-	Peregrine Darkin before 1717, brother of Mark, an innkeeper 1679-1691, wife Elizabeth. Peregrine his wife & children in Old Newton 1662 - 1664 & 1683 "late Stowmarket now in Chelmondiston"
unkn-	Thomas Marriott, but before 1709
1711-	Martin Howsen
unkn-	Henry Martin, but before 1717
1713-1719	Robert Scarlett, paid 3/9d tax in 1713
unkn-	Thomas Brooke & wife Elizabeth before 1721
unkn-	Thomas Peck, but before 1721
1735-	Samuel Robinson
1749-	Thomas Marriott

1750-	John Martin, innholder living in Battisford
1762-	Robert Bone & Robert Scarlett jnr
1768-1770	Samuel Pratt
1779-1791	Samuel Elmer, 1789 fire destroyed wash house/store room stable & 3 adjacent cottages
1791-1794	Widow Elmer
1794-1815	Thomas Kemball, he married Martha Elmer in 1795, Thomas died 1815
1815-1834?	Martha Kemball, break-in 1816 nothing taken, quit rent 1837
1834-	John Wilden
1835-1840	Thomas Eastwick, died 1840 aged 54
1841-	Jabez Hobart
1844-	Robert Ellis
1846-1853	Thomas Wells, aged 66 in 1851
1855-	Thomas Webb
1856-1864	Isaac Gillingham, 33 yrs in 1861, fined 1861 open out of time, had his watch stolen 1864
1865-1876	Edward Youngs & wife Sarah, a cattle dealer, age 30 in 1871, fined £2/5s in 1874 for selling out of hours, rent £10 p.a. he won breach of warranty case in 1875.
1876-1886	William Abbott, & pig jobber age 34 in 1881, died 1886
1886-1887	Mrs Emma Abbott, she married George Greengrass, see next entry
1887-1890	George Greengrass
1890-1903	George Copsey, age 53 in 1891, died 1903
1903-1915	Mrs Fanny Copsey, retired to Bridge Street with her brother Charles Byham (her manager) she died in 1925
1915-1925	Thomas Shepherd
1926-	Augusta Amelia Shepherd
1926-1952	Frederick John Baker
1952-1957	Harrold John Syrett
1957-1960	Thomas Robertson Parker
1960-1971	Derek Lionel William Baker, died 1971
1971-1974	Susanna Baker, widow of Derek, she died 1974
1974-	Robert F & Daphne Turner

1974-1977	C P Owen
1978-1983	Colin J Morgan
1984-1987	Donald J Clemson
1988-1991	Michael Taylor
1992-	Duncan Darbyshire
1993-1996	Jonathan Hewitt & friend Melanie A Scott
1997-	Jonathan Hewitt tenant
1998-2000+	Melanie A Scott.

MAYBUSH
43 Bury Street
c.1838 – 1922

After closure

The Maybush was one of the many beerhouses which sprang up in the town from the 1830s onwards, trading from just one or two rooms in a family house. Occupier James Clarke lived here from 1836, he is listed as a beerseller in an 1839 directory; he also worked as a brazier, possibly at the nearby firm of James Woods, they produced mainly agricultural equipment.

There was a grocery shop on the premises by 1851, the occupier is often described in the census as a beerseller and shopkeeper. The house consisted of three rooms downstairs, two cellars, and a jug department for off sales, four bedrooms and a kitchen.

The Brett family owned and ran the beerhouse from 1871 to 1896, firstly Frederick a former hop gardener & on his death his son John. They were followed by Catherine widow of John. A few years before her death at the age of 73 in 1899 Catherine sold the property to Morgan and Co. the Norwich brewers. Francis and Elizabeth Shaw came to the Maybush at this time, Francis had worked on the land for most of his life but took up inn keeping sometime in the 1880s and ran the Bedingfield Arms in Eye. He had also served as a parish clerk for his home of Ixworth Thorpe for 21 years. Alice their daughter ran the Maybush with her mother after Francis's death in 1905, and on her own after her mother died in 1920. The building was demolished in the early 1970's along with the garage (Scarff's then Wright's) next door, and the whole site was redeveloped for housing. NL

Owners

1839-1843	Richard Webb, bricklayer
1844-1847	Mary Ann Webb
1847-1859	James Williams
1860-1870	John Lummis
1871-1871	Frederick Brett
1871-1882	John Brett, 1879 fined, no gun licence
1882-1896	Mrs Catherine Brett
1896-1922	Morgan & Co. Brewery

Occupiers

1838-1839	James Clarke, brazier
1840-1861	William Tricker, a cooper, married 56 years to Sarah Webb my ancestor (BAS)
1862-1870	John Lummis
1871-1882	John Brett, 1872 theft from
1882-1896	Mrs Catherine Brett
1896-1904	Francis Shaw
1905-1920	Mrs Elizabeth Shaw
1920-1922	Alice Shaw
1922-	Closed

MILLERS ARMS
Thorney Green Stowupland
Before 1842 - c1872

After closure

In 1815 farmer Thomas Bauley was the owner of the windmill on Thorney Green. In 1842 the Stowupland churchwardens paid him for supplying wine, he is still listed as a miller/beer retailer in Kelly's directory for 1846, however he had passed away in 1844 aged 63. His son Dennis continued as miller/beer retailer until his own sudden death in 1848 aged just 40. Second son George took over and ran the business until 1864. I suspect two nephews ran the mill while George ran the beerhouse.

The next change was in 1865 when a Charles Warner is listed as miller/beerhouse keeper, Charles & his wife Martha were involved in a court case in 1872 when they were charged for selling beer "out of time" the case was however dismissed, but their licence was refused soon afterwards. A Charles Thomas Warner (the son?) was buried in 1872 aged 34 years, the beerhouse seems to have closed at this time, but the mill continued for some time. BAS

NORWICH ARMS/ OLD NORWICH HOUSE
17 Ipswich Street
c.1850 – 1908

c.1909 after closure

William King cabinet maker/upholsterer the owner of this property since about 1850 sold it in 1858, just when it became a beerhouse is a little uncertain. The next occupier in 1855 was James Ives a 45 year old shoemaker, subsequently he became the owner, living with him was his brother in law 31 year old Arnold Suttle. After the death of Ives in 1866 at the age of 50, Suttle, a general dealer & former landlord of the Royal William purchased the Norwich Arms. His advert was placed in the Stowmarket Courier in July 1869 " To put up at Michaelmas next a public house doing good trade, wine & spirit free & the coming in moderate. The yards & premises are extensive & an advantageous business has been carried on in connection with the house which will go with it" wonderful archaic phrasing! The purchasers were Alexander Clutterbuck's Stowmarket Brewery (see elsewhere). The change of name occurred in 1879 during John

Alexander Cook's tenure. In 1882 Edward Greene & Co were the owners, eventually merging to become Green King. The licence was declared as unnecessary in February 1908. Four years after closure there was a suicide, George Easlea aged 18 years of Old Norwich House was found hanging. The building was later to become Walkers Stores (renumbered) & was demolished in July 1972. BAS

Occupiers

1850	Robert Tricker & baker/confectioner, if a beerhouse
1851-1854	William Bevan at an unnamed beerhouse, also a butcher
1855-1865	James Ives & shoemaker, open beyond hours fined 10/- unnamed beerhouse
1865-1866	George Leathers, enrolled 1865 6th Sffk Stow' Rifle Vol' Corps, 5ft 6½, age 32
1866-1869	Thomas Pooley
1869-1876	John Aldous, a horse dealer age 31 in 1871, late Royal Wm, 1876 assaulted, to the Bell
1876-1877	Arthur Brook(s)
1877-1881+	John Alexander Cook, a boiler maker, wife Julia A, his son was hurt on the railway. John won a court case in 1879
1883-1885	Romanus Brown, interim licence
1885-	Edgar Sheppard, charged with assault, case dismissed
1885-1886	John Reynolds
1886-1893	John Cook & drayman, gave evidence in court case, died at pub 1893 age 41
1893-1896	Mary Ann Cook, age 38 in 1891, widow of John
1896-1898	Owen Poll
1898-1908	Thomas Ward, a whitesmith (died 1934 aged 78, ex fireman 40 years)

PICKEREL
65 Stowupland Street, formerly in Stowupland
Before 1565 – current

The Reverend Arthur George Hollingsworth wrote in 1843 his version of the history of Stowmarket, he states that the Pickerel in 1565 was used as a house of reckoning on the annual feast day. I can find no other information on it's existence until 1763 when the will of Robert Marriot of Thorney Hall was proven. Situated near the banks of the river Gipping where pike no doubt swam the structure is listed as of circa 18th century, but it would seem to be much older than this.

A William Rushbrook senior of Stowupland, innkeeper, was buried in 1676 & a William is on the 1666 hearth tax, whether he was at the pub is anyone's guess, information for Stowupland is not so forthcoming as for Stowmarket. The Marriot family continued as owners, John (eldest nephew of aforesaid Robert) in 1798 & John (another?) in 1847 & 1855. The Stonham Brewery in the form of it's owner John Keen Sedgwick were the next owners in 1859, his trustees managed the property after his demise in 1866. A part owner from around 1869 to 1881 was a Joseph Owen, he was an Ipswich bank manager so it would seem the pub was mortgaged. On or shortly before 1873 Catchpoles Brewery of Foundation Street in Ipswich purchased the pub, eventually in 1923 they sold out to John Cobbolds Brewery, the annual rent in 1923 was £1,030 (£42,000).The national brewery chain Pubmaster became owners and in November 2003 they sold out to Punch Taverns.

One particular landlord of the past was John Baker; in 1868 he admitted owing his suppliers money & was jailed, he was examined for bankruptcy in 1869 with debts of £213 (£14,700) with assets of £14. A serious fire in a building next to the bridge destroyed the thatched stables of the pub' in 1874, the loss was about £300. In 1877 Baker lost another court case concerning non-payment of monies, in the same year he was arrested on a charge of stealing corn, was remanded and served 9 months. Despite all this Baker had his licence renewed, why? well perhaps it was because his father in law was none other than John Lockwood, he was the former owner of the Fox Hotel & a farmer on the Bury Road. The next landlord was Henry Gooding, he came from Barking Lion & his occupation was that of boot & shoemaker. In 1879 he opposed local grocer Thomas Dent's application to sell beer by the bottle, also in this year his son Harry saved a boy from drowning in the nearby river Gipping. Gooding purchased 4 red brick residences in 1893 for £460; he promptly let them out. It was reported in the Stowmarket Weekly Post of December 12th 1905 that, "Colour Sergeant G Wright of the Suffolk Regiment at Bury St Edmunds, will shortly be posted to Stowmarket as recruiting sergeant with HQ at the Pickerel, Wright is a native of Stowmarket".

The venue was certainly used for parish meetings around the 1820 period. Two daring robberies were reported in the Ipswich Journal, the first in 1907 and the next in October 1911. Bobby George the TV darts personality visited the pub on January 25th 2005. Over several years the Pickerel Yard was a resting place for many travelling families. BAS

Occupiers
1666	William Rushbrook, unconfirmed
1772	an estate sale to be held at the Pickerel
1780	William Leathers, a house sale, unconfirmed landlord
1798-1800	Thomas Thing landlord, he died there
1800-1802+	Mrs Sarah Thing, married widower Wm Smith in 1802

1804-1806	Samuel Smith innholder, of Pickerel died in 1806 age 62
1811-1825	Simon Robinson, died there age 54
1825-1841	Ann Robinson, nee Ann King of Tostock age 69 in 1841 (married Simon Robinson 1808)
1844-1847	Samuel Pulham
1850-1858	William Theobald Corner, died there age 42
1858-1861	Mrs Mary Ann Corner, widow age 45 in 1861, married John Lockwood 1862, see the Fox
1861-1865	James Warne, from Bury St Edmunds
1865-1877	John Baker, age 43 in 1871
1877-1893	Henry Gooding, age 52 in 1881
1896-1897	Walter Baker
1900-1901	George Henry Aldous, age 45 in 1901
1902-	Arthur Gillett Ramsey
1904-1914	Edgar Thomas Ramsey
1914-1915	Albert George Moss, court case, no conviction, not drunk
1916-1921	Frederick Borrett, fined £2 for supplying a soldier liqueur
1922-1924	Herbert William Blazier
1924-1956	Charles William Norman, wife Lily died 1954 age 73
1957-1973	Edward Finbow, wife Edna was the daughter of Charlie Norman
1973-1979	Arthur E C Finbow
1979-1984	Keith W Palmer
1985-1989	Thomas A Paton
1998-	Bob Fleming, manager for John Collins of Stowupland Crown
1999-	Michael Porter, manager for John Collins of Stowupland Crown
1999-2000	Carol Gwilliam landlady
2001-	Richard Jordan. Jasmine Chima & Elton Baker, Jasmine formerly of Punch Bowl/Stowupland Crown.

PHOENIX TAVERN
25 Station Road
1886-1921

The Phoenix Tavern isn't the first hostelry to exist on this site, that honour belongs to a beerhouse owned by Robert Worledge a Debenham born tailor. Robert ran his tailor & drapers shop from about 1858, and by 1864 he had added a boot and shoe warehouse, this was turned into a beerhouse by 1869. A collision of traps (horse & traps) in September 1880 left Robert with fractured ribs. He passed away in 1885 aged just 55 years; he is buried with his wife who had predeceased him. Shortly afterwards his executor's put his tailors shop & licensed beerhouse up for sale, it was however withdrawn at £250.

In June 1885 there occurred one of Stowmarket's most serious fires. Mr Dent's grocer's shop on the corner of what was then Stowupland Street and Station Road was completely destroyed, "the flames spread along the roof and speedily wrecked a beershop and tailors shop which stood next door" this beautiful complex of houses was a great loss to the town. Soon afterwards Oliver John Parker (owner of the Unicorn in Lime Tree Place) rebuilt 25 Station Road, but the area from the corner up to the newly built property remained an un-saleable eyesore for some seven years until Parker also rebuilt the corner shop, (later Stannard's cycle shop and subsequently Codd's cycle shop) and 27 Station Road (Chelsea House) in which he lived until his own untimely death in 1904.

James Lillistone was born in the Bakers Arms in Violet Hill Road in 1861, the ninth child of Charles and Sophia Lillistone. James's profession was that of baker. He spent one year as landlord of the Vulcan Arms, and by October 1886 he was the occupier of 25 Station Road. Just exactly when he named his beerhouse the Phoenix is unclear but a quote from him in 1890 says, " I went to the hole in the wall which became the Phoenix". The pub was always known as the hole in the wall due to it's small size.

We know of a few more incidents from the early life of James, in May 1885 he enrolled in A company Stowmarket Rifle Corps and is described as being 5 feet 6 inches tall. In August 1897 he was assaulted and in June 1901 a fire was caused when filling a small spirit stove, his children were burned but he was able to quench the fire. In July 1902 two local men Caley and Pryke were charged with stealing 8/6d from the till shortly after Mrs Lillistone had served them.

Following the death of Mrs Parker widow of Oliver and sister of James Lillistone the property was put up for sale at the Fox in May 1910, the freehold Phoenix public house with 7-day licence and tobacconists shop adjoining with 6 rooms was purchased by Lillistone for £800. Always a man to heavily promote and expand sales, James in 1919 submitted plans to take the small front window out of his sitting room to enable him to display his tobacco wares. Today if you look carefully you can still see where this window has been put back in the intervening years. The part that was the Phoenix closed in 1921 but James went on to a long and interesting life. (See Serving You Through The Years by Sue Cowling and Steve Williams for much more on James Lillistone).

James seems to have named his beerhouse because it had arisen phoenix-like from the ashes of the old beerhouse, but he was at one time very involved in the Phoenix Lodge of Freemasons........ BAS

POT OF FLOWERS
also known as the Flowerpot and from 1831 to 1844 as Tyrell Arms 90-92 Bury Street
1707 - 1978

The building that was the Pot Of Flowers is now two private houses 90 & 92 Bury Street, still with the name above one of the front doors. The building is listed and is described as early 18th century.

The Dictionary of Pub Names mentions the Stowmarket pub and also a Flower Pot in Hounslow and Cheriton. It suggests that the Flower in the original sign of such inns was the Lily associated with the Virgin Mary. This may indicate a pre-reformation origin for Inns of this name, and that later the emphasis was put on the pot rather than the flowers, and indeed the Stowmarket Pot Of Flowers is often referred to as the Flower Pot in 18th and early 19th century documents. There is no indication however for a date that early for this inn. The first record of the building is a deed of 1707 between bricklayer Mark Wright of Stowmarket and Mark Wright the younger of Stowupland, grocer, presumably father and son. Mark Wright the elder as a bricklayer may well have been the builder of the Pot Of Flowers possibly on the site of an earlier building. The building is described in this document as,

"three messuages then two in Haughley Street [as Bury Street was then known], *abutting upon the messuage of the late Timothy Folkard* [a blacksmith who died 1705] *and then of George Richardson, and upon the messuage sometime of John Keeble and then of Robert Rosier to the North".*

The name Pot Of Flowers does not appear in this document but between 1711 and 1714 Robert Mixter appears in the overseer's accounts as paying poor rates for a public house by the name of the Flowerpot, he is also listed as licensee in the notebook of Devereux Edgar in 1714. Also in 1714 and 1715 Thomas Birch and Daniel Thorpe paid poor rate for "part of the Flowerpott" so the building must still have been 2 separate houses.

On the death of Mark Wright the premises described as *"a Common Inn called the Pot Of Flowers with 2 other tenements adj."*, passed to the ownership of Nathaniel Fairclough, and he or his son in 1762 mortgaged the property to Rev. Garnham of Bradfield St.George. Fairclough died soon after and in 1764 Elizabeth Spencer purchased *"The Flower Pot & 2 tenements adjoining"*. Elizabeth Spencer dying in 1780 left the Pot Of Flowers to George Clemens & Eleanor his wife & then to their children or John King their nephew, worsted weaver. George Clemens died in 1802 and the following year the pub and a stable situated opposite was sold to John Aldrich, brewer of Stowmarket and owner of a number of other inns in the town. He immediately advertised the property in the Bury and Norwich Post as *"annual rent very low, £10, good stabling, Bowling Green, Several large clubs, entire business of two day Lamb Fair"*. The meadow where the annual Lamb Fair was held was on the opposite side of the road as was the bowling green mentioned. It seems to have been usual for the landlords of the Pot Of Flowers to rent this meadow from the Parish of Stowmarket for their own use for the rest of the year.

Clemans had died in debt and a further notice in the Bury and Norwich Post appeared assigning debts of G. Clemans to John Howe of Wetherden, liquor merchant & John Aldrich, brewer. But Aldrich had debts of his own and in 1805 all his inns and property in the town were handed over in lieu of debts to £12,000 to his father in law, John Cobbold, brewer of Ipswich.

Henry Ungless was now the landlord of the Pot Of Flowers. Ungless had been associated with several other inns in the town. He was at various times at the Swan and the White Horse and the White Hart. Vestry minutes of this period show that the Town Rents were then collected at "The Flower Pot". The expenses for the churchwarden's refreshment here in 1804 came to – *"wine 2s, punch 2s, brandy 2s, rum 4s, hollands 2s, tobacco 1s, liquor etc. 5s"*.

In 1831 the Pot Of Flowers changed it's name to the Tyrrell Arms, the name reverting to the Pot Of Flowers in 1844. Harry Double in one of his books on Stowmarket gave the location of the Tyrrell Arms as the premises which is now Jon Simon hairdresser in Bury Street. Evidence from rate books shows the Pot Of Flowers and the Tyrrell Arms were actually the same building. The use of the name of the prominent local family the Tyrrells of Gipping Hall and Stowmarket may have been an attempt to change the pubs image and go "up market". As with some modern day attempts to appeal to a different clientele by changing the name and image of the establishment this seems to have been unsuccessful or unpopular and the name reverted to the original.

A later tenant, Samuel Pope gave evidence in 1902 when the motor manufacturer Frank Lanchester was fined £5 for furious driving in Stowmarket; he was estimated to be travelling at 16-18mph!

Many local people still have fond memories of the pub, Dudley Diaper recalls that -
"It was the haunt of the Sixth Form of the Grammar School when I was in it, 1967-1969. Those with a bit of pocket money would congregate in the Lounge bar on Friday nights and mostly drink either Tolly Cobnut (sweet brown ale) or stout and cider mixed, as none of us was very fond

of Tolly bitter. The favourite chair was an old cinema seat in the corner. The licensees were very friendly and tolerant of us "boys" and even turned a blind eye if we took in the odd bottle of home-brew when our money ran out. After a fairly long drinking-up time it was over the street to Norman's for chips on the way home. There was a private room, which we occasionally hired for a party. On the wall was the headdress of the Royal Antediluvian Order of Buffaloes.

In 1972 a few years before closure a tragic incident took place when Alfred Coe shot and killed Mervyn Lawrence Chumbley. Chumbley had been drinking at the Pot Of Flowers and had got a message to meet Coe in the nearby car park where the shooting occurred. Chumbley was able to stagger back to the door of the pub where he was discovered by Edwin Hill, the landlord.

It emerged at the inquest that Coe had befriended Chumbley who had lived with him and his much younger wife Mary at their home in Top Road Rattlesden; indeed they had both been charged with stealing copper and were awaiting trial at the time. Chumbley and Mary had become friendly and she left her husband for Chumbley. After the shooting armed police called at Coe's house, they heard a shot as they broke in and found Coe dead, shot through the forehead. NL

Owners

Before 1707	Mark Wright, bricklayer
1707-17??	Mark Wright, grocer
1731-1754	Nathaniel Fairclough, tanner
1754-1756	Elizabeth Fairclough, widow of Nathaniel
1756-1763	Nathaniel Fairclough junior
1763-1764	Elizabeth Ottey, daughter of Nathaniel Fairclough
1764-1780	Elizabeth Spencer
1780-1802	George Clements
1803-1805	John Aldrich
1805-1978	John Cobbold and then Cobbold and Co. brewers

Occupiers
1711-1715	Robert Mixter
1715-1719	Thomas Birch, later at the Angel
1731-1732	Sarah Spencer, wine licence
1732-1748	William Spencer
1748-1780	Elizabeth Spencer
1780-1802	George Clements
1804-1808	Henry Ungless
1814-1817	Peter True
1817-1820	Thomas Girling
1820-1830	William Smith

As Tyrrell Arms
1831-1843	William Smith
1844-1844	Ann [Nancy] Smith

Reverts to Pot of Flowers
1844-1850	Ann Rice [previously Smith]
1849-1855	John Broom, previously at the Bell and later at The Carpenters Arms
1856-1859	Benjamin Colman
1859-1861	James Williams [previously of the White Lion]
1861-1864	Edward Payne
1864-1881	Abraham Diaper, shopkeeper/cattle dealer
1881-1906	Samuel Pope, sawyer, carpenter, undertaker, sewing machine agent
1906-1915	Herbert James Oliver
1915-1925	Walter Joseph Montague
1927-1949	Mrs Florence Maud Montague
1949-1956	William Tracey Good
1956-1975	Edwin Charles Hill [previously at the Rose]
1975-1976	A. E. & D. E. Hawes
1977-1978	Mrs Doreen. E. Hawes
March 1978	Closed

PORTERS LODGE
35 Stowupland Street

After closure

The house and other adjoining property was in the hands of the Codd family of Haughley from at least the mid 18th century. In 1789 George Codd [see the Barge] sold the building to Webster Adams. There were Websters in five successive generations of this family and this particular Webster was probably the 2nd of that name. He is described as a pipemaker in 1789 an occupation followed by many members of this family over six generations. Many broken clay pipes have been found on the land to the rear of the house.

In 1828 the property was left on Webster Adams death to his nephew Robert Folkard Adams. Webster II also had pipemaking interests in Ipswich and owned the George Inn in Needham Market. A probable landlord from c1836 to 1839 was James William jnr; he then went to the White Lion.

In 1848 the house was bought by James Earthy Godbold who describes himself at that time as farrier and beerseller, so it would have been from this time that the use of at least part of the building as a beerhouse dates. The origin of the name is unknown; maybe it was popular with porters from the nearby station.

James must have gained a knowledge of horses through his work as a farrier because he later describes himself as a veterinary surgeon. The old stable in which John shod and treated horses is still standing at the rear of the property and there is access from Union Street previously known as Cats Lane. A small cellar under the floor of one of the rooms in the house may have been connected with brewing or the storage of beer.

The house remained in the hands of the Godbold family until about 1940. NL

POTASH
Upper Combs
Before 1779 - 1799

Possibly situated at Pot Kiln Farm. All the information on this beerhouse comes from the overseers account books.

1779-1782	Abraham Smith an outsitter, the owner?
1786-1792	Rev John Freeman owner? he died 1792 aged 47, a rector of the Creetings
1793-1802	Rev Orbel Ray owner? (he lived at Tostock & was related to the Oakes banking family).
1779-1782	Francis Mayhew occupier
1785-1793	John Boon occupier, also at the Punch Bowl from 1773 to 1789
1793-1799	George Ward occupier.

BAS

PRINCE OF WALES
Ipswich Street
[previously the Falcon]
c. 1859 - 1907

Second from right - after closure

The owners of this beerhouse from 1859 were Henry Cuthbert and John Hart Bridges. As Bridges Cuthbert & Co Ltd and then Bridges & Co the company operated a brewing business in Ipswich named the Falcon Brewery after Falcon Street in which it was situated, hence the original name of this beerhouse in Stowmarket.

Right from the start it seemed unprofitable, the many short-lived tenants having a variety of other occupations, being situated adjacent to the Royal Oak probably did not help.

It stayed in the hands of Bridges & Co. until 1873 when another brewer, William Golland Ranson took over ownership. Golland, originally from Cambridgeshire came to Stowmarket as the Station Master in the early days of Stowmarket station. Later he traded as a coal merchant, malster and carting agent and also opened a brewery in Violet Hill Road, obtained the ownership of several local pubs and beerhouses.

In 1896 Ranson sold off his public houses and Tollemache Ipswich Brewery became the next owners, they remained as such until it's closure in 1906. The building was described at this time as having "entrance porch, bar, tap room, beer store & pantry, sitting room, kitchen or club room, 4 bedrooms, cellar, yard with door to Church Lane, and which is a building formerly a fish drying house, now a washhouse, water closet etc. also a urinal in Church Lane" Two previous tenants had been fishmongers which accounts for the fish drying house.

During the 50 years of it's existence the Prince of Wales had over 25 different tenants! Most stayed no more than a year or two, so it was no surprise that the beerhouse was one of the first to close in the wave of closures brought about by the 1904 Licensing Act, the aim of which was to reduce the number of pubs by offering owners and occupiers compensation.

We do however know more about the decision to close the Prince of Wales as the documents relating to this have survived.

At the annual licensing meeting held at the court house on 5th March 1906, the licensing authority objected to the renewal of this licence on the grounds that there were more licensed houses in the area than necessary.

John Foulger Page, the superintendent of police stated that part of the premises which had previously been the taproom had been recently converted into a butcher's shop. The following statistics were quoted to support the case for closure: -
In 1901 the population of Stowmarket was 4,162 of which 2,358 were over 15 [the age limit for entering a public house]. This number was catered for by 27 licensed premises or one to every 106 persons. As the women included in this number would not have been considered to have used the pubs nearly as much as the men the actual ratio was in reality even lower.

In Ipswich Street there were 5 other premises within 150 yards of the Prince of Wales and one, the Royal Oak was right next door.

The conclusion was that there was not sufficient trade and the beerhouse was unnecessary for the requirements of the populous. The building is now a take away food establishment. NL

Owners
1847-1858   George Collen a plumber, bankrupt, not a pub?
1859-1873   Henry Cuthbert (of Diss) & John Hart Bridges
             [Falcon Brewery]
1873-1896   William Golland Ranson [Stowmarket Brewery]
1896-1906   Tollemache Ipswich Brewery

Occupiers
1859-1859   James Girling
1860-1861   Edward Spaul, blacksmith
1862-1864   E. Davey, 1862 F Tricker knifed by G Ames
1864-1864   G. Moor
1864-1865   G. Wood
1865-1866   Thomas Liddy, 1865 in Sffk Rifle Vol' Corps 5ft 11"
             aged 40
1866-1867   James Welham
1868-1869   James Miller, tailor
1869-1873   Thomas Pooley, fishmonger, pub damaged in Gun
             Cotton explosion.
1873   name changed to the Prince Of Wales
1874-1874   Henry Sillett, fishmonger
1875-1876   Edward Baker
1876-1881   James Hammond
1881-1881   Israel Lambert
1881-1889   Henry [Harry] C. Talbot,
1889-1890   James Ramplin
1890-1892   Albert Mullins, basket maker, 1890 wife Alice gave
             evidence in court case
1892-1892   James Halls, his widow Mary Ann gave evidence at
             his inquest
1893-1894   Abraham Thornally 1894 fined
1894-1896   Walter Henry Brooker, born Colchester Essex,
             frontage of pub 30 feet
1896-1897   Gyles Rivers

1897-1899	Walter Fox
1899-1899	Reuben Simpson
1899-1900	Charles John Dalby an Ipswich man, 1900 fined for serving out of hours
1900-1904	Stephen Rushbrook, 1902 indecent exposure case
1904-1906	Charles Woodrow
1907	Closed

PUNCH BOWL
Upper Combs (now Battisford)
1727 - current.

c.1895

Built by Ambrose Wright on a meadow that he had bought for £50 from John Bogges of Great Finborough, this beerhouse is still in existence. The original name was the Sweep Chimney & remained so until it's sale for £100 (£15k) in 1732 to Josiah Winter of Little Blakenham. In his will of 1749 proven in 1752, he leaves part of the Punch Bowl to his son Josias Winter, the other part was to go to Anne Hayward & Edmund Stearns. However, the partners promptly sold out to William Aldrich, he owned many inns & pubs in the area (see his story elsewhere). After William Aldrich passed away in

1767 all his property went to his son, also William. Six years later the Punch Bowl was owned by Charles Aldrich the third generation of the family, he was a London draper & was still the owner in 1788. A John Aldrich followed from 1797 until 1805 when he sold out to John Cobbolds Brewery.

Here are details of an auction sale in 1790 of departing occupier/butcher John Deves "feather beds, pewter, brass, chairs, tables, chests of drawers, good clock in wainscot case, two coppers, one ditto & mash tub for brewing of four combs of malt, a kitchen coal range, crane & hooks, about two tons of hay, useful mare, two cows forward with calf, 3 two year old steers, one cow with calf by her side". BAS

Occupiers

1727-1732	Ambrose Wright & owner
1746	Petty sessions held there, signed John Green
1747	Petty sessions held there, signed Samuel Turner
1748	Petty sessions held there, signed John Edgar
1751-	William Ward, petty sessions held
1762-	William Adams
1773-1789	John Boon/Bone, windmill sale held there 1776
1789-1790	John Deans or Deves
1790-1792	William Pegg, deceased sale of his goods
1792-1844	John Makings/Meakins etc
1850-1863	Sarah Meakins daughter of John/Mary age 43 in 1861; rent in 1857 was £12 p.a.
1851-1853	Mary Meeking, age 85 in 1851, died 1853 widow of John, she was landlady 61 years, her descendants were at the Staff of Life/Barge/Stowupland Crown.
1864	Isaac Dickerson in Kellys
1864-1892	Maurice/Morris Dickerson, & farmer, age 27 in 1871, son of Dennis/Rebecca, fined 1871. His wife Elizabeth drowned herself in 1874.
1891-	Dennis Dickerson in census, youngest son of Dennis/Rebecca
1895-1903	William Dickerson son of Maurice, he sued the landlord of Needham Market Rampant Horse over an accident in 1899, split judgement, fined 1903 for permitting drunkenness, his licence not renewed.

1903-1941	Frank Cobbold, he died there 1941
1941-1977	Cecil Thomas J Cobbold then he retired, was born in the pub 1904
1977-1981	Albert M & Sandra F A Smith
1982-	Roy A Fell
1983-1985	Campbell V Pearson
1986-1989	Steven M Cooper
1990-1992	Ann P Trayler
1993-	David R Bumstead
1994-	Henry W Golightly
1995-1996	James W Faredon
1996-1999	Steven F Schulen
1999-2000	Lorraine Schulen, nee Mattin
2000-	Jeff & Jo Fields
2000-2005+	Mr & Mrs Lewsey, they purchased it from Pubmaster in 2001
2006-	For rent. In September 2006 it was purchased by Provedence Investment Co & reopened at the end of 2006.

BELL/QUEENS HEAD
Bury Street

We have an excellent account of this ancient building, this stems from an advertisement in the Ipswich Journal of 1858, sadly this was the end of a pub that had started off it's life in the 29th of Henry VIII i.e. 1538. Walter Manning clothmaker of Thorpe & late of Stowmarket, sold the newly built house the Bell in Haughley Street (Bury Street) to three Stowmarket men, these were John Thorpe, John Godard & John Fish. It was next to a property owned by John Fish, now this John had already in 1536 taken delivery of a large consignment of wine from Tooleys of Ipswich. By large we know that it amounted to more that 1,764 gallons, perhaps he was stocking up for the grand opening! The will of John Fish was proved in 1552, however he is not buried in town. The recently transcribed hearth tax returns for Suffolk reveal that in 1666 (lady day) the house late the Bell was empty, it had 5 hearths, so was of a generous size. This is the last found reference to the pub as the Bell, as in 1679 the registers reveal that two soldiers died at the Queens Head. Why was the Bell renamed? well I suspect that the new bride for King Charles II was the reason, Catherine of Braganza became his wife in 1662. We know the Bell became the Queens Head because fortunately a transcript of a mortgage of 1688 survives, John Keeble of Stowmarket to John Acton of Bramford for £400 (some £60k today) of the Queens Head formerly the Bell in Haughley Street. This property had previously been mortgaged to Daniel Bigsby of Crettingham for £300 at some unknown date; Daniel had married in town in 1676. The exact time period the next few owners took over is unclear, indeed as above they may well have had only a small interest in the property. Richard Keyan gardener of St Helens Ipswich took over before 1709; he was followed by Thomas Read. In November 1716 John Harvey gent of Colchester insured the premises. We know that before 1736 Martin Webster was the owner followed by Charles Barnwell of Norfolk, he sold his interest to William Bunn, now Bunn is better known, he stayed from 1736 until his death in 1750. Incidentally the rent in 1737 was 6/10d p.a. Bunn's son in law William Aldridge owned the business from 1750 until his death in 1767 aged 66. The story of the Aldridge/Cobbold line is told elsewhere. That concludes the ownership story that can be ascertained at present.

The exact position of the Bell/Queens Head has puzzled us for many years, it seems to have been on what is now the traffic light junction, & next to what was until 2008 Hamilton Smith Estate Agents, i.e. the road was narrower than we know it today. We have several confusing location details but the best comes from the Bury & Norwich Post of July 4th 1805 "positioned on the corner of Ipswich Street, Bury Road & Stowupland Street (now Station Road) & opposite Finborough Road" (Tavern Street). However the poor rates of 1814 seem to put it in Stowupland Street.

Another problem that has eluded a solution is the exact date that Cobbold built his new Queens Head it would seem to have been between 1850 when John Cobbold mortgaged it & the destruction in 1858 of the old building. Now for an account of the old building as seen in two adverts in the Ipswich Journal. " For auction at 2 o'clock on Wednesday December 20th 1857 the old Queens Head. All the excellent timbered house known as the "Old Queens Head" situate near the Church, containing bedrooms, parlour, kitchen, washhouse, backhouse, extensive cellarage; all the doors, windows, capital brick & wood flooring, with all the beams, jowls, girders, of old English oak, pantiles & plain ditto etc. The whole will be sold in one lot, & to be taken down at the purchaser's expense, & removed immediately; the whole to be cleared away 21 days after the sale. The sale will commence with the tenants fixtures, comprising register stoves, kitchen range, shelving etc. A catalogue will be produced at the auction with conditions etc" The next advert found states " To be sold by H S Downing (auctioneer) on Monday March 3rd 1858. All the valuable building materials arising the pulling down of the old Queens Head comprising fine old English oak beams & plates of large sizes, 80 capital floor joists, 7 X 5 inches sound & well suited for carving, with superior panelled & other doors, sash windows with frames & shutters, hearthstones & doorsteps, chimney pieces etc, see catalogues" BAS

Occupiers of the Bell/old Queens Head

1683-1709	John Lucas?
1709-1712	John Nunn, suspect.
1713-1714	Elizabeth Lucas.
1716-1719	George Taylor & wife Mary (maybe later).
1719-1725	Andrew Spence ?
1728-1733	Mrs Sarah Spence widow.
1734-	William Stedman.
1735-1738	John Broom.
1738-1740	Robert Rodwell.
1740-1762	John Nunn, Benjamin & Elizabeth Shipling an elderly couple live at the pub.
1762-	Richard Willet.
1763-c1766	Abraham Southgate.
1766-c1780	Thomas Flood, a tailor also takes over adjoining shop, large stock men's/boys clothing, violently assaulted 1768, reward offered.
1780-1782	Lewis Hunt, to let ancient & spacious inn, large yard good stables.
1791-1793	Riches Fox, retired, declining health.
1793-1804	William Ward.
1806-1807	Abraham Thurlow & cabinet maker. 1806, from the diary of John Green Crosse "went to the Queens Head to see Mr Coans wonderful performance in cards, balancing, tumbling & hornpipe dancing".
1809-1812	John Rowling, chimney fire 1811, to be let 1812.
1812-1817	George Ranson from Crown & Anchor Ipswich, bankrupt 1814. Coach service to Bull Inn Aldgate in 1814.
1817	April & July unoccupied.
1817-1821	John Smith, to let apply Cliff Brewery, John to the White Horse.
1821-1834	Samuel Bird.
1836-1837	Shadrach Sparrow.
1837-1838	Eliza Quilter.
1839-1842	James Quilter, age 55 in 1841, wife Sarah.
1842-1844	Edward Barrett, & boot & shoemaker.
1844-1847	Mrs Eliza Barrett.
1848-1850	James Quilter

QUEENS HEAD
Station Road

As discussed in the Bell/Queens Head the new building may have been completed about 1850. It's is very typical of Cobbold's many new properties of the period & fortunately it has survived in what was it's original design. On July 27th 1916 the war office conducted a survey of all accommodation for horses in the country, the Queens Head had room for 60 horses in it's 8 stalls.

1967 leaving party for A. E. Ames

The Queens Head as such, closed on February 18th 1997, it reopened to a select few on May 21st 1997 & named Capones, with the full opening the next day. Happily when Michael Prentice took over sanity was restored along with it's original name "THE QUEENS HEAD. BAS

Occupiers

1850-1866	Charles Williams, & tax collector, aged 47 in 1851, to let £10
1866-1882	William Game, age 54 in 1871, a horse race reported 1878, his son at Dukes Head in 1892
1882-1899	John Thurston, age 36 in 1891, fined for breaking contagious diseases act 1890.
1899-1906	William Syer Ling, age 25 in 1901, assaulted in 1906.
1906-1913	Percy Jennings, ex sewing machine agent, first boxing club formed in 1908.
1913-1934	Joseph Arthur Oliver, buried 1936 age 72, see Stowmarket Recorder.
1934-1954	William Fish, on electoral roll there in 1930, wife Dorothy, he died 1963 age 82.
1954-1957	Ernest Robert Pells.
1957-1967	Arthur Edward Ames, moved to Ireland.
1967-1975	Richard H Hammond.
1976-1980	Sidney A & Edna Painter.
1980-1997	Robert (Bob) C. Osborne.
1997-2000+	Jonathan Hewitt tenant for Pubmaster.
2007-	Michael Prentice landlord for QUEENS HEAD.

RAILWAY TAVERN/HOTEL
Station Approach
c. 1847 - 1978

c.1906

Stowmarket Station was opened on Monday 7th December 1846 and the first train from Ipswich, Colchester and London ran on the 27th December calling at Stowmarket on it's way to Bury St. Edmunds. Frederick Barnes station building was not completed however until 1849. The arrival of the railway resulted in an increase in the number of licensed premises in this part of the town.

The Railway Tavern opened by 1847 and was in Stowupland parish being on the north side of the river, which at that time formed the parish boundary between Stowmarket and Stowupland.

Originally named the Railway Tavern and Refreshment Rooms, the name the Railway Hotel was adopted in 1888 when Tollemache acquired the brewery and pubs of Charles Cullingham & Co. including this building. It's position opposite Stowmarket Railway Station meant a steady trade and a series of long tenancies through the second half of the 19th century would suggest a good living could be made here.

The landlords here seldom seem to have a second occupation although John Martin was a farmer in Onehouse; he had also been at the Rose and the White Horse in the town. Amongst his effects on his death were a hackney mare, and a greyhound. A survey during W.W.I. showed that the hotel had stalls for 7 horses. The building was later used as a dog-grooming parlour and is now a children's pre-school playgroup. NL

Owners
1847-18??	William Barnsley Fairs
1854-1858	J. Cuthbert of Stonham Brewery
1858-1865	J.K. Sedgwick of Stonham Brewery
1866-1866	Sedgwick's trustees, owners of Stonham Brewery
18??-1888	Charles Cullingham & Co. Brook Street Brewery
1888-1978	Tollemache & Co.

Occupiers
1847-1850	Edward Mullet, inquest
1851-185?	Eldred Howes, age 42
1853-1867	Thomas William Bloomfield, his furniture for sale 1867
1875-1875	John Martin, Onehouse farmer, was at Rose & White Horse, fined 1870 selling out of hours, died of bronchitus, wife died 3 months later, 1870 his furniture sale, hackney mare, brace greyhounds.
1875-1877	Samuel Charles Bloomfield
1877-187?	Mrs Bloomfield
1879-1885	William Burnett [interim licence]
1888-1909	James East, 1900 burglary at hotel
1909-1910	Josiah Shipp, previously 20 years at Bildeston Kings Head
1910- 913	Mrs Mary Ann Shipp
1914-1917	Walter Ward
1917-1919	Mrs Mary Ward, 1917 husband in army
1919-1921	Walter Read Ward
1921-1921	Mary Evelyn Ward
1921-1927	William Edward Moores
1928-1955	Melville Garner Pinner
1955-1961	William Steggell Collier
1961-1963	Alfred Henry Albert Manning
1963-1965	Henry William Parker, then to an off licence in

Brightlingsea
1965-1968   Clarice A. Devereaux, formerly of Burlington Café
             Needham Market
1969-1969   Clarice [formerly Devereaux] & Louis F. Monks
1970-1971   Albert J. & Kenneth J. Allard
1971-1973   George "Tex" & Miriam Butler, formerly
             chauffeur to Billy Smart
1973-1974   Bruce Ketley
1977-1978   Arthur Brown, to Feltham Middlesex
3rd Aug 1978 Closed

RED LION
5 Tavern Street
c.1853 – c.1910

Time was finally called at the Red Lion in 1910, during it's some 50 years of trading it did seem to retain the landlords somewhat longer than was usual for a beerhouse.

The first owner that has been found was William Clarke, he also owned the next door property occupied by Samuel Bridges the coach-makers, however by 1858 Clarke had sold both properties to Bridges. Samuel retained ownership until his death in June 1858 at the age of 44, his widow Mary Bridges owned the Red Lion until 1871, by this time she would have been 60 years of age. Her son Harry Bridges followed her; he was born c1839 & was the owner until Edward Bridges took over in 1883. The rate books of 1884 have no owner recorded for the Red Lion, but by October 1885 the Steward & Patterson Brewery had taken up ownership.

Here are a few observations on some of the landlords. Robert Cuthbert a shoemaker, his son Henry was killed in the Zulu War when 15,000 warriors attacked his regiment. Robert was for more than 50 years a Stowmarket bellringer; he died in 1868 age 66. The next landlord was carpenter Albert Cooper; he married Mary Anne Cuthbert the daughter of his predecessor. The couple produced at least 7 children of whom 5 died; they & their father are buried together. George Southgate was my great great uncle, a basket-maker by trade he only obtained an interim licence. Walter William Peart a millwright was charged with assault in 1901 the case was dismissed. William James Brightwell was convicted of assault on his wife in 1906. In 1909 referred for compensation, "he pays £10 p.a. rent" Arthur S Leighton appeared for owners Steward & Patterson, claim was for £341-5s, (£25,500) offer made & referred to the Inland Revenue. The property is now a dentists, and is appropriately painted red. BAS

Occupiers
1853-1868	Robert Cuthbert
1869-1875	Albert Cooper
1875-1880	Henry Welham
1880-	R Elliott interim licence
1881-1886	Thomas Waller Ward, a fishmonger, age 51 in 1881. Was assaulted by 3 men in 1882
1886-	George Southgate, interim licence (my great great uncle)
1887-1887	Mrs Eliza Luen
1887-1889	Henry (Harry) Cable, a dealer from Wherstead Rd Ipswich
1889-	Roland Ward
1890-1902	Walter William Peart "Red Lion must be suitably troughed" died 1902 age 59
1902-1904	Mary Ann Peart, buried 1904 age 61
1904-1910	William James Brightwell, son in law of Walter Peart.

RETREAT
Thorney Green Stowupland
pre 1854 - 1969 Old Retreat, 1969 - current New Retreat

The original Retreat was housed in a thatched barn-like building; it was said to be 300 years old when it was vacated in 1969, unfortunately like many old buildings that perhaps should have been preserved, it was demolished.

The first account I can find of the owners was in January 1854 when Stevens & Co trading as the Stowmarket Brewery were at the Retreat. Stevens sold out to Phillips Brothers (still trading as the Stowmarket Brewery) in 1865 for £240, this included two tenements. Furthermore in 1874 the pub including a cottage was sold to the then landlord Edward Palmer for £530. In 1882 Edward Greene of Bury St Edmunds purchased the property, eventually merging to become Greene King in 1887.

After a succession of landlords the old Retreat closed it's doors in February 1969. The newly purpose built Retreat opened on February 14th 1969 & Rowland A G James & his wife Marjorie moved from one Retreat to the other. BAS

134

<u>Occupiers</u>

1852-   Foyster Howlett innkeeper of Stowupland was married, Retreat?

1854-1855   Henry (Harry) Raffe un-named beerhouse, buried 1857 age 73

1858-1862   John Miller at Retreat, a fowl dealer, age 33 in 1861. Fined after a quarrel in 1861

1862-   Mrs Powell

1863-1866   Robert Wilden, fined 1863 & 1864 for serving out of hours

1869-1881   Edward Palmer, & fowl dealer age 40 in 1881. Fire in thatch of fowl-house 1875

1881-1883   Thomas Stebbings, fined 10/- 1883 ill treatment of a pony

1883-1888   Henry Soames, see Staff of Life 1904

1888-1924   George Frederick Wilden & poultryman, fined for allowing horses to stray in 1904

1924-1966   Leigh Wilden, married 1925 to Gladys Lillian Pettit. Publican's licence in 1960

1966-1969   Rowland A G James

NEW RETREAT

1969-1983   Rowland A G James, works at Suffolk Lawnmowers, Miss Greene King visits 1972

1983-   Marjorie I P James

1984-2000+ Michael W Hawkins

ROSE
5a Buttermarket
pre 1645 – 1958

Situated in the small street leading from the Market Place to the Churchyard now known as the Buttermarket, but at one time this was where the butchers set up their stalls or shambles.

The Rose was the nearest inn to the church, the association of inn and church goes back to medieval times so we may expect it to have had an ancient origin. There was until recently a date (1461) painted on the gable of the building. It is not known if this was when the building was erected, but it is the opinion of an expert in timber framed buildings that the core is of a 15th century date, there are also wall paintings in this part of the building possibly from the 16th century. The first documentary record we have found for an inn named the Rose is in the will of Robert Brasier of Bramford of 1645 in which he left the Rose to his brother Edward. A Robert Brasier was baptised in the town in 1604 and his brother Edward in 1600.

There are a number of mentions in churchwardens accounts to show that the Rose would have supplied beer and wine for various church events, as in 1662 when "Beere was payed for at the Rose for the soulgiers" when the Bishop of Norwich came to inaugurate Samuel Blackerby as Vicar of Stowmarket. Soldiers were also billeted at the inn during the epidemic of 1679 when two soldiers died here.

The Inn was still in the Brasier family in 1683 when John Brasier a miller of Bramford left it to his son John.

Beer was supplied for other celebrations as in 1699 when Roger Wheeler of the Rose provided "a visel of bere for haysil [haymaking]" to Daniel Mulliner of Howegate Farm Stowupland. The Inn briefly came into the hands of the Cobbold family when the owner John Rust's daughter Ann married the Reverend Thomas Cobbold, this was not the brewing branch of the family however and it was not until 1862 that Cobbolds again owned the building. There are stories about prisoners being held in the cellars of the inn but these are unsubstantiated, if true this may be connected with the County Assizes being held in the town in the 17th century.

Today it houses the offices of the Stowmarket solicitors, Gudgeon and Prentice. In the reception the old bar counter has been retained. NL

Owners

16??-1645	Robert Brasier
1645-16??	Edward Brasier
16??-1683	John Brasier, miller
1683-16??	John Brasier junior
1692-1699	Roger Wheeler
1701-1707	Robert Pett, draper
1708-1714	Jeremiah Bigsby junior
1714-17??	Stephen Bacon
17??-1742	Daniel Bacon
1742-1747	Daniel Ling
1761-1763	Robert Marriott
1763-1775	John Rust
17??-1778	Rev Thomas Cobbold

1778-1783	Samuel Manning
1783-1798	Robert Marriott
1798-1853	John Marriott nephew of Robert Marriott
1854-1861	John George Hart
1861-1862	Executors of J. G. Hart
1862-	John Cobbold brewer

Occupiers

1605-1678?	perhaps Scalpy family, John, Thomas & the widow
1678-1692	Lawrence Fuller, then to the George
1692-1697	Roger Wheeler
1714-1714	John Jennery/Chenery
1714-1718	Robert Mixer/Mixter
1718-1719	Daniel Wright
17??-1741	Samuel Fisher
1742-1748	Daniel [?] Ling
1766-17??	Edward Dyson, draper
1777-1783	Samuel Manning
1798-1799	John Betts
1812-1815	John Smith
1815-1832	Robert Smith, butcher
1833-1833	Mrs Smith
1834-1834	Francis Dale, died 1834 struck by lightning
1835-1835	Ruth Dale widow of Francis married Robert Thorns of Onehouse
1835-1841	Robert Thorns maltster, 1839 was paid 17/6d for celebration of the Queens confinement, to White Horse
1842-1850	Owen Whayman, vetinary surgeon
1850-1851	Robert Smith junior, died aged 27
1851-1854	Elizabeth Cullum & son Edward
1854-1854	Mumford & Chapman wine and spirit merchants or their tenants
1855-1855	Nathaniel Thurston Codd, earlier of Kings Head
1855-1862	John Martin tailor, then to White Horse & Railway Tavern
1862-1900	James Hartwell Dawes, 1871 fire, wife Caroline died aged 36, he remarried, 1900 knocked down by a dog in his back yard & died from head injuries some 9 months later. Originally from Rushmere.

1900-1900	Harriet Dawes widow of James
1901-1945	Arthur Wilfred Tarrant son in law of James Dawes. Tarrant's wife Harriet Maud died aged 35.
1945-1949	Jessie E. Tarrant 2nd wife of Arthur
1949-1956	Edwin Charles & Eileen Hill, then to Pot of Flowers
1956-1957	Arthur Edward Ames, then to Queens Head
1957-1958	John Knight Thomas Webb, then to the Warwick Woodbridge
1958	Closed

ROSE AND CROWN
Stowupland, location unknown

Very little is known about this establishment, it is a possibility that this became the Crown, but somehow I doubt it. The only reference to it is in Devereux Edgar's notebook, a Suffolk JP he conducted his survey & names it in April 8th 1714 when a John Porter was there. A John Porter of Stowupland was buried in 1715 & another in 1740. BAS

ROSE AND CROWN
32 Bridge Street
c.1867 - 1992

1992

Carrier William Turner is the first known occupier of this beerhouse, this was in 1867; the house had been built a few years before. By 1869 William had retired, he was about 74 years of age & the carrier business & beerhouse were in the hands of his son Joseph. Judging by the cemetery records he & his wife lost at least 9 children over a ten-year period, this brings home to us the terrible death rate of the time, & seems to have been due to the lack of proper sanitation in the town. Joseph Turner stayed until late 1874, & during this early period of the pub it seems to have had 3 owners.

John Edward Bellchamber a 46 year old tailor was the initial owner in 1861 until 1871. Clerk, accountant & house agent Henry Payne followed until late 1874. The next year was a pivotal one in the story of the Rose & Crown, for in 1875 George Diaper a Stowupland born man purchased the business & with his wife Florence built up the trade & is listed as shopkeeper & brewer. Just when he started the adjoining Crown Brewery is hard to judge, but certainly by 1888. The pub had from it's inception taken in lodgers & this continued until the First World War. In 1897 Diaper applied for & was refused a full licence, just over a year later he died & was described in his obituary as a gentleman aged 54 years. In 1900 the rate books have Diapers executors as owners, this is crossed out and "Page" inserted, soon afterwards Greene King became the owners.

In 1957 a fixtures & fitting valuation was carried out by Woodward & Woodward prior to the new landlord, we can therefore see the number of rooms etc "parlour/bar/taproom/lobby/kitchen /storeroom/cellar & 4 bedrooms". A publican's licence was eventually granted in 1960. Another inventory of 1978 gives us further insight to the running of the property. The gaming licence worked out at 2.28 pence per day, the fruit machine made a profit of £714 (£3,000 today) over a twenty two-month period. Further interesting items were "2 shove halfpenny boards, 3 wooden pegging boards, 1 copper faced peg board, 3 boxes of dominoes, bristle dart board, a dart sharpening stone, set of poker dice in a leather shaker, 2 spare poker dice, 2 sets of darts, 3 cherry B goblets etc". The gross profit over the twenty two month period was £9,409, (£39,000) so we can see that hard work & long hours paid off & the retiring landlord was able to purchase a house in Lockington Road. The old Rose & Crown is now (2009) a supported accommodation for people with head injuries. NL/BAS

Occupiers

1867-1868	William Turner
1869-1874	Joseph Turner & Caroline, were in town c1864
1875-1898	George Diaper & Emma, from the Walnut Tree
1898-1903	James Walker Calver/Carver & Fanny, a saddler age 39 in 1901
1903-1917	George Thomas Felgate, a coach trimmer age 40 in 1901
1917-1920	Harry Kerry, died 1922 age 47, Garnham here in 1920 see next entry
1920-1921	James Parker Garnham & Harriet, maybe lodgers
1922-1933	Horace Kerry, a thatcher, to Claydon Crown
1934-1957	Charles Edward Ford Wilden, retired to 47 Bridge

Street, brother of Leigh of the Retreat.

1957-1978	Donald Charles Wilden (son of above) & Betty
1978-1984	Frederick J Buckingham
1984-1992	Peter L & Margaret Coleman, moved to Unicorn the next day (3rd July).

ROYAL OAK/OAK
43 Ipswich Street
c.1824 - current

Strictly speaking this pub started off life as a wine & spirit store, an advert' by owner merchant Samuel Henry Wright in 1870 has the legend "established in 1824" & shows an oak tree. The first known owner was Robert Aldrich, he commenced business in September 1828 & was a Stowupland gentleman farmer & auctioneer, and he put the Oak up for sale in 1841. John Mumford in partnership with Thomas Sheldrake were the next owners until c1852, when they were joined by John Everett Chapman. However in 1853 Thomas Sheldrake passed away aged 58, his long & successful time in town started in

1822 when he took over a grocers/drapers shop from Pearson Till. Chapman's partnership with John Mumford lasted until 1866 when the following advert' appeared in the IJ

"For sale the entire household furniture of John Mumford, a messuage, a garden having an extensive frontage next to Ipswich Street, used as an Inn or retail wine & spirit house with counting room, bottle stores, sitting & bedrooms in occupation of John Mumford & John Everett Chapman. An extensive wine & spirit trade has been carried out for many years"

From about 1879 until 1888 Chapman had a retail wine & spirit outlet in the Market Place, this was located where Barclays Bank is today. However his home from c1851 to c1882 was The Limes in Ipswich Street, he then moved to the Ashes in Newton Road. Samuel Henry Wright was the Oak's owner from 1866 until his death in 1886 at the age of 57, he was born in town in 1839 where his parents ran a Saddle & harness business in Tavern Street. Samuel had started in the trade with Stevens' Stowmarket Brewery as a commercial traveller in wines & spirits, he never married. In 1883 he was secretary of the Freemasons, after his death his executors ran the business until 1900. The next owner was Cyril C Tuck; this was from 1901 until the death of his 33-year old wife in 1906. Tuck was a busy man, he was a banker's clerk, secretary of the Corn Exchange, a Captain in 2nd volunteer Suffolk Battalion A Company, an insurance agent & rate & tax collector. His various addresses were; Fasbourne Villa Finborough Road (his mother's), 71 Ipswich Street, Milton House Ipswich Road & Russell House Ipswich Road. The Oak's next owner from 1907 to c1913 was an A. M. Page, & a Mrs Page is shown in the 1911 valuation list as an owner. In 1937 at Stowmarket there was a burial of an Alice Margaret Page, she was brought from 15 The Grove Finchley N3 aged 82, she would seem to have been the previous owner of the Royal Oak. By 1916 the Green, King brewery had bought the Oak & used it as a bottle store as well as a retail outlet. BAS

Managers/innkeepers
1861-   Robert E Burroughs innkeeper
1881-   Oliver Holden wine merchants assistant age 37 at
                   Royal Oak
1882-   Mr Wright's traveller Mr Barnard hurt in accident

1886	Nov 24th James William Leggett manager
1887	Dec 15th Mr Barnard manager, Elijah Barnard traveller, to at least 1901.
1886	Dec 15th Eliza A Grimwood to carry on wines/spirits (dept'?) as before (IJ) widowed sister of Samuel H Wright, there in 1871.
1891-1907	John Thomas Flowers clerk/manager, age 15 in 1891
1907-1909	Ernest Robert Cross, a fruiterer, died 1909 age 34
1909-1911	Robert Charles Palmer, protection order 1909, 6 day licence granted 1909
1912-1921	Oliver Charles Robert Parker, born c1878 son of Oliver of Unicorn, fined for permitting drunkenness in 1914
1921-1923	Albert Edward Evans
1923-1954	Frederick William Woodroffe manager, closed Sundays
1954-1959	Gordon Campbell Donald
1959-1962	Reginald Henry Miller
1962-1963	Cyril Rosewell, 6 day licence removed
1963-1971	Alfred Allchin & Doris, he was cleared drunk driving 1966 age 53, to Wethersfield Tavern
1971-	Bernard & Joyce Harrison, from Ipswich
1972-	Graham Mitchell
1973-	Peter Ernest & Patricia, left suddenly after threats of violence, court case
1974-	George H Houghton
1974-1977	John E & Thelma J Cox
1978-1980	Richard A Darlow
1980-1981	Martin & Susan Wiegand
1982-	Electoral roll blank
1983-1984	Anthony G Tilbrook
1985-2000	Chris & Ellie White
2000-2002	Trevor Theobald, to Little Wellington
2003	renamed the Oak.

ROYAL WILLIAM
53 Union Street [formerly known as Cats Lane]
c.1837 - present

A small back street local that like so many started life as a beerhouse in the wake of the 1830 Beer Act. Many of these beerhouses were closed down in the early 1900s but the Royal William probably owes it's survival to the fact that there were no other licenced premises close by. It achieved a full licence in 1962. The beerhouse was originally part of the Paul estate. The Paul family had been brewers in Foundation Street Ipswich but later concentrated on malting, Robert Paul who had family connections with several Stowmarket businessmen including James Woods and Robert Hewitt founded the company R. & W. Paul in 1842.

Later it became part of the Stowmarket Brewery Estate throughout the breweries various owners, before passing to the Bury St Edmunds brewery of Edward Greene, later Greene King.

Robert Chapman who kept the pub for some years at the end of the 19th century also had a market garden and played in the local silver band. Today it is one of the towns few remaining old-fashioned pubs, occasionally playing host to the local Morris dancing team. NL

145

Owners

1837-1838	Robert Paul
1838-1840	Francis Paul
1842	For sale with unexpired lease by Unicorn Brewery Ipswich
1851-1853	Farrow
1853-1854	Robert Paul [part owner]
1855-1857	John W. & G. Stevens
1857-1874	Phillips Brothers leased by them until 1865 when they bought for £280
1874-1882	Alexander Clutterbuck [Stowmarket Brewery]
1882-1887	Edward Greene & Son
1887	Greene King

Occupiers

1837-1853	William Smith, cattle dealer, age 46 in 1851
1853-1855	Arnold Suttle late of the White Lion
1855-1856	Walter Brand
1856-1863	Edward Rodwell, tailor
1863-1864	William Freston, fined 1863
1864-1864	William Wright
1864-1869	John Aldous, later to the Norwich Arms
1869-1885	James Adams, carpenter previously of the Carpenters Arms
1885-1901	Robert Chapman, also gardener
1901-1912	William Emmerson
1912-1912	Jane Emmerson
1913-1914	Daniel Halls
1914-191?	Jane Emmerson
1916-1917	George Davy
1917-1920	Mrs Annie Davy [husband in the armed forces]
1920-1929	George Davy
1929-1951	William Sturgeon
1951-1958	Reginald Colin Lambert
1958-1970	Oliver William Robinson, public licence upgrade in 1962
1971-1972	Robert Ezra & Robert J. Savage from Ipswich, 1971 music licence
1972-1985	George Henry Scott
1986-1991	Geoffrey P. James
1991-1997	Phillip G. Rudland
1998-2000	Stanmuth O. Young

SHIP
Stowmarket, location unknown

1710?	Edward Brazier owner, sells to William Kent of Woolpit.
1712	By his will, William Kent tallow chandler of Woolpit owner.
1713	Probation of will Wm Kent, leaves the messuage or tenement commonly called or known as the Ship to Susan Taylor with conditions. Now in occupation of James Cook (born 1654) & others.
1714	Not on licence list. BAS

SIR JOHN BARLEYCORN
117? Lime Tree Place

The name barleycorn has many connotations. A grain of barley was the beginning of our measure of length, the third part of an inch. There was also a popular song by this name & it is a personification, often humorous of strong drink.

The Morris Suffolk directory of 1868 lists Robert Proctor (born c1816) as a beer retailer & shopkeeper, also the 1869 Stowmarket Courier has the information that Proctor had applied for a certificate for the Sir John Barleycorn, the case was adjourned for 14 days. Later in that year it was reported that he was assaulted. In 1870 Proctor re-applied for a certificate for the beerhouse, again this was refused, also in 1870 a fire at the rear of the property in a stable used by Mr Bethell was reported. No further references to this beerhouse have been found. He stayed at the shop until about 1882 when the Holden family occupied the premises & traded as grocers until just before World War Two. BAS

STAFF OF LIFE
26 Stowupland Street
Pre 1836 - Closed – 1911

After closure

The Staff Of Life was one of the beerhouses that sprang up around the middle of the 19th century as a result of the Beerhouse Act, and closed in the early 20th Century in an attempt to limit the number of pubs in a particular area.

Bread is said to be the staff of life, but thanks to a drawing of the sign by Edward Edwards in the early 1880s we know that a lump of cheese and a jug [presumably of beer] were depicted along with a loaf. Another version of the sign was said to have included "the 3 b's" beer, bread and beef.

Edward Edwards was a solicitor who for recreation travelled around the country in a donkey cart sketching, he mostly sketched inns and their signs. He published these in large quarto volumes, engraving the illustrations and text himself, a real labour of love! He came to Stowmarket on his travels in 1883 making several sketches. One of these shows the signs of both the White Lion and the Staff Of Life together.

No doubt the beerhouse like the Barge just a few yards away, it catered for trade from the Gipping Navigation and the men who worked at the maltings and warehouses that grew up beside it.

The building seems to have been a shop before it's life as a beerhouse. From 1836 to 1849 it was owned by J. Cobbold the Ipswich Brewer, that suggests it may have been a beerhouse from the earlier date and possibly back to 1830, the date of the Beer Act which created the beerhouse. William Colson was tenant there in the early 19th century and he appears in a directory of 1830 as a shopkeeper and is later referred to as a shoemaker. In 1849 Colson purchased the building from Cobbold and was the owner from then until his death in 1856. John Colson, a son of William and also a shoemaker took over the premises on William's death. The premises stayed in the hands of the Colson family until John's death in 1871 brought a change of owner and occupier. Charles Woods of the small Bacton Brewery based at the Bull in that parish was now the owner, and the licence passed to Frederick Barnard who stayed on until 1879 when he moved to the Horse And Groom in Station Road. He was followed by a Robert Wilden and on his death in 1883 by his widow.

The Hammond family of Old Newton were here from 1886 to 1905. William Hammond later went to run the Retreat at Stowupland, being summoned for assault there on a number of occasions. At it's closure the Staff Of Life was in the ownership of Eugene Wells.

After it's demise as a public house the premises were sold to Charrington's brewery for £150 and divided to form two houses, the Ward family lived at 26 & 26a for many years, the property was then owned by E.W. Hart who ran a butcher's shop on the corner of Union St. and Ipswich Street. [See the Stag]. Lesley Ward recalls the house as he knew it ....
"Harold William Ward my grandfather first had this house when we lived in both 26 and 26a Stowupland Street We then moved into 26a. We then all moved back into both sides when my father married. The present kitchen was the pump room when the building was a pub & the present front room was the bar. To the right of the door going from the front room to the kitchen was a serving hatch. On some of the panelling

around the front room you can still see where the bench chairs and tables once were. You can just see some letters of people carving their names in the wall. The cupboard in the front room was a passage way though to a snug or lounge of the pub. The front bedroom, cupboard and box room were the bedrooms of the guests staying at the inn, and the front bedroom of 26a was for the staff of the inn. The old bar had a brick floor, but was cemented over in the 1920's. It had a large fireplace, which was open to the snug supplying heat to the bar and snug. In the garden, stood a bottle store which held big stone jars of beer etc." NL

Owners

1836 - 1849	J. Cobbold
1849 - 1861	William Colson & executors
1861 - 1871	John Colson
1871 - 1872	Mrs W. Colson
1872 - 1885	Charles Woods
1886 - 1887	Eugene Wells
1887 - 1907	Thomas Prentice & Co
1910 - 1911	Eugene Wells
1911	Charringtons Brewery

Occupiers

1814 - 1856	William Colson, a shop in 1830
1856 - 1871	John Colson
1871 - 1872	Mrs Louise Colson
1872 - 1879	Frederick Barnard
1879 - 1883	Robert Wilden, heart disease died aged 48
1883 - 1886	Mrs Sarah Wilden
1886 - 1904	William Hammond, 1902 summoned for assault by Henry Soames of the Retreat, police objected to the licence renewal in 1904.
1905 - 1908	Robert Fulcher, 1908 fined for permitting drunkeness
1908 - 1908	William Henry Gladwell, died 1908 had come from Needham Mkt
1908 - 1909	Emily Gladwell widow of William, two men stole from her just 3 weeks after the death of her husband,
she	died at the pub a few months later.
1910 - 1911	Andrew Arthur Gladwell son of the above.
19/8/1911	Closed

STAG TAVERN
44-46 Bury Street
c.1982 – current

The Stag Tavern is at present the newest in a long line of Stowmarket pubs going back over 500 years. However this concern has had a complex set of owners. Starting with Gabriel Anthony Martin Gibney, he purchased what at one time had been Harts the butchers in 1981 for £35K, (£97K) he was then living at Angel Hill Bury St Edmunds. In July 1982 a mortgage with the Greene King Brewery was secured for £5K. Then in 1985 Gibney a publican of Northgate Street Bury St Edmunds entered into an agreement with Melvyn Douglas Shaw of the Stag Tavern. In February 1986 a further mortgage for £10K was obtained from Greene King. Gibney sold his share of the property in 1989, possibly to Lydia Ketteridge who is listed as owner at the same time as Melvyn D Shaw until 1998. Patrick & Bridget Murphy owned the tavern from 1997 until 2003 & were operating their microbrewery from 2001 with the expertise of master brewer John Palmer. Managers ran the Stag Tavern some of the time, those known are Eric Joyce in 1988-1989, Stephen A Searle 1990-1996, Philip G Rudland in 1998. The Stag Tavern was sold to Punch Taverns in 2003. BAS

SWAN
Bury Street
c.1542 - ?

In 1542 William Sabyn in his will left a property called "the Swan" to his nephew. In 1653 Richard Collyngs tenant of the manor of Abbots Hall sold his tenement called the Swan otherwise Dryvers in Hawley Street [now Bury Street] to one Thomas Leman.

There were later inns in the town named the White Swan and Black Swan but this inn being in Bury Street seems unconnected with them. NL

TANNERY
Hadleigh Road (now Park Road) Combs

A short-lived concern this beerhouse and gardens were owned by the Rev Richard Daniel in 1864. The occupier was William Mattock from c1864 until his death in 1871 at the age of 48. Quite often a widow carried on with the business and this was the case, as when Maria Mattock was granted a licence and continued until she was made a bankrupt in 1876. An interim licence was granted to Zachariah Southgate (newspaper has John) but was opposed by his neighbour George Webber of the nearby Live and Let Live beerhouse. Zachariah was born in 1831 and was a thatcher by trade, he continued with the beerhouse until as least 1883. I believe he died in 1906. BAS

THORNEY GREEN BEERHOUSE
Stowupland

All we know about this beerhouse is from the following advertisement that appeared in the Suffolk Chronicle for September 9th 1857. "Lot 1, Freehold dwelling houses, beershop & cottages Thorney Green Stowupland to be sold by H S Downing (auctioneer) at the Kings Head, Stowmarket, on Thursday September 17th (by order of the director of the trustees of the late John Wells deceased). A substantial brick built freehold dwelling house & beershop, with a yard & garden, fronting the high road leading from Stowmarket to Mendlesham, where a good beer trade had been carried on for many years. Late in the occupation of John Wells deceased, also a freehold dwelling house with yard & garden adjoining in the occupation of James Diaper at a yearly rent of £5. Lot 2, Four freehold tenements, or cottages, with yards & gardens well planted with choice fruit trees, adjoining Lot 1, and in the several occupations of Robert Berry, Joseph Cooper widow Sheppard, & Thomas Baxter. Annual rental £13-15s. F Hayward solicitor Needham Market".

John was probably born in Stowupland in 1777, he can be found on the 1841 census in Thorney Green Road with his Norfolk born wife Charlotte, where his occupation is given as a carter. By 1851 his address is Gipping Road, and his occupation is given as a house proprietor aged 74 years. John was buried in the Stowupland churchyard on July 9th 1857 age 81 years, his wife Charlotte was buried with him on February 27th 1861, aged 82 years. BAS

TWO BREWERS
Bury Street (see Vulcan Arms)

In 1876 the property was owned by brewer William G Ranson, by this time the probable landlord Thomas Welton had gone. In 1877 the Ipswich Journal had an advert " to let with shop and bake office, immediate possession apply William G Ranson". BAS

UNICORN
24a Lime Tree Place
1861 - current

Originally built as a bake house by local builder Thomas Cook in 1860, although just why master builder Ephraim Rednall is listed as the first owner until 1865 is rather puzzling. However brewer H J Bridges of the Violet Hill Brewery was the next owner, he put it up for sale unsuccessfully in 1865. He tried again in 1867 "For Sale, freehold property, new premises a beerhouse & bake office, comprising 2 recently erected dwelling houses, having neat white brick front elevations, a good cellar, bar, large sitting room, pantry, kitchen & bake office, 4 bedrooms, yard & gardens, now in the occupation of Simon Suttle at an annual rent of £16". The pub was sold for £1,050 (£65,500) including 3 adjoined houses to a Samuel Pullham, but by 1870 he placed an advert in the Stowmarket Courier. "To be sold at the White Lion on Friday June 24th eight freehold private dwellings in Lime Tree Place, a public house with bake office attached & a large plot thereon now used as a carpenters shop & timber yard". This did not produce an owner because in March 1871 the freehold beerhouse was sold to Mr Cook for £260; the property was being let to Phillips Brothers Stowmarket Brewery.

The adjoining property was a separate residence with a baker's shop in the downstairs front room; the actual bakehouse formed part of the rear of the beerhouse. This property has now been incorporated into the pub & the front door to the baker's shop made into a window. The next owner/occupier seems to have been James Leeks (see Duke of Wellington) he is described as a retired shopkeeper age 33, unfortunately he died in September 1876. In December that year his widow Charlotte applied for a licence, however it was withheld until "communication stopped" with another person who used the bake house. Charlotte married Oliver John Parker in June 1877, Oliver was described as a seedsman & Conservative agent, he was some 8 years younger than his wife, the couple stayed until 1897. Oliver was the son of Robert a former landlord of the Greyhound & owner of the newly built Phoenix beerhouse in Station Road. He became it's owner (presumably upon his father's death) & proceeded to build Chelsea House & what was later to become "Codds Corner". The Unicorn was sold to Greene King for £3,500 in January 1897 "an unheard of price". NL

Landlords

1861-	Mrs William Palmer, bakehouse only?
1861-1862	Samuel Pope, & builder, beerhouse licence granted 1861, to Pot of Flowers in 1881.
1863-	Edward Matthews
1863-1864	Frederick Green, beerhouse & baker
1865-1871	Simon Suttle, a lathe render age 48 in 1871, to Combs Volunteer Arms
1871-1876	James Leeks & owner
1876-1877	Charlotte Leeks & owner
1877-1898	Oliver John Parker, sued for assault 1892 & 1904
1898-1913	George Scipio Riches, to Claydon Crown
1913-1914	Harry Pizzy, temporary transfer
1916-	George Scipio Riches again, Pizzy is in next door shop
1920-1948	Harry Pizzy, wine/sweet licence 1948, was a cornet player Sffk Reg' died Jan 1949 age 73
1948-1964	Cecil John Mayhew, upgraded to pub licence 1964, was previously the baker at the rear of Unicorn, wife Ruby ran shop next door, she died 1964.
1965-1990	Lionel W Barnard
1991-	Anglia Innkeepers
1992-2000+	Peter L & Margaret Coleman.

THE VOLUNTEERS
Poplar Hill, Combs Ford
c.1861 – 1913

Combs Village.

Several companies of volunteer militia existed locally, part time soldiers, similar to today's territorials. Originating at the time of the Napoleonic wars when the fear of invasion was very real, they would muster a few times a year to drill and no doubt retire to a local pub afterwards. Whether this particular beerhouse had any connection with any volunteers is not known. On its sale in 1866, stables, 5 cottages and some arable land are also mentioned.

The most colourful landlord at the pub was undoubtedly Alfred Potter. Born in Stonham Aspal in c1829 he followed his father as landlord into the Volunteers. In 1863 he got a young lady pregnant, he was about to marry her when she changed her mind and married another. In an 1870 court case he tried to recover two shillings from a Henry Palmer for damage to a wheelbarrow, also in the same year an assault case was reported. Catchpole's Brewery ordered him to quit the pub in 1872.

After it's closure in 1913 Charles Hubbard bought the old pub and converted it to a butchers shop, I well remember just after the war taking the cleaned potted meat jars back to him for a deposit refund. The building was eventually demolished in 1980. NL/BAS

Owners
1863 - 1866   J.K. Sedgwick [Stonham Brewery]
1866 - 1866   H.J. Bridges
1866 - 1913   Catchpole and Son, brewers of Union Brewery
              Foundation Street Ipswich

Occupiers
1861 - 1863   Joseph Potter, aged 60 in 1861
1863 - 1872   Alfred Potter son of Joseph
1869 ?   Robert Bridgeman, charged with keeping open out
              of hours
1872 - 1885   Simon Suttle, previously at Unicorn
1885 - 1889   Alfred Bugg and Mrs Bugg from Whitton previously
              at Cow and Pail Ipswich, 1889 court case, they owed
              money
1891 -1900   Robert Boast
1901 - 1903   Edgar and Mrs Dearing [daughter of Robert
              Bridgeman]
1903 - 1913   Thomas Edward Robinson, gardener
              Refererred to compensation authority & closed 1913.

VULCAN ARMS
37 Bury Street
c.1864 - 1913

John Potter on left

The position of this beerhouse very close to James Woods' ironworks seems likely to have been the inspiration behind it's unusual name, Vulcan being the roman god of fire and metal-working. The foundry workers no doubt frequented it. In October 1875 a fire at Woods' Suffolk Iron Works "threatened Mr Woolnough at the Vulcan Arms, wet blankets were applied to the projecting gable end, whilst neighbours assisted Woolnough to remove his furniture". Woolnough had an eventful life, after leaving the Vulcan Arms he was employed as a coachsmith at the nearby Holt Carriage Works. In 1882 he was burnt with hot steel, and at his inquest it was stated that he had been "a member of the fire brigade, a forester, and leaves a large family". So fire in one form or another formed a large part of his life and death.

There appeared an advert' in August 1896, this gives us an invaluable insight as to the size of the pub, "house built of brick and plaster, plaintiled and slated, a lobby, bar 13 x 6 feet, tap room 13 x 9 feet, scullery 16 x 15 feet, a side passage way, 4 bedrooms, a yard with one stall stable, and an outhouse".

The Ipswich Journal of March 23rd 1901 gives a comprehensive account of the trial of Thomas Makens a 39 year old Stowmarket drover; he tried to kill Mrs Emeline Smith wife of the landlord. In a nutshell, he attempted to strangle her with a rope after making improper remarks to her. Nearby butcher Philip Metcalf cut the rope and freed her. The police were sent for, and Mabel Beaumont daughter of Arthur the landlord of the Kings Arms gave evidence. The prisoner was committed to the assizes. Mrs Smith admitted she had accompanied Makens to two other public houses in the past. Makens had previously used violence to ravish women. The jury found him guilty of attempting grievous bodily harm; the sentence was 18 months hard labour.

By February 1912 the Vulcan Arms was referred to the compensation authority, Mrs Maria Potter the wife of landlord John said "he was afflicted", however John lived at this address until his death in 1927. BAS/NL

Owners
1865-1868   William Beard
1869-1874   Mrs William Beard
1875-1896   William Golland Ranson, brewer
1896-1913   Tollemache, brewers

Occupiers
1867-1868   William Beard
1869-1877   Nelson Woolnough
1877-1879   William Sutton
1879-1881   William Gardiner of Combs then went to Buxhall
1881-1885   Arthur Thomas Peck, interim licence, a brewer
1885-1885   James Lillistone, "I was there for a twelve month" & to the Phoenix
1885-1885   Arthur Ellis
1887-1887   James Durrant from Haverhill
1887-1888   Thomas Ward, interim licence. See I/J 9/6/1881.
1888-1895   Sarah Ward, widow/shopkeeper, had pony & trap stolen 1888, previously at Red Lion, later at Bakers Arms
1896-1901   Fred Smith
1901-1913   John Potter
1919   Building bought by W & C Simpson from Tollemache

159

WAGGON AND HORSES
Navigation Wharf Stowupland

From 1842-1846 the landlord was George Codd, before this he was at the Barge, he died in 1860 aged 87. The foundations of the railway station are possibly on land occupied by part of the Thorney Hall estate and the Waggon and Horses. This was possibly over the Station Bridge on the left side. By 1889 a butcher named William Botting lived in a house called the Old Tavern, the rate books suggest this may have been on or near the old pub. By 1898 William had become a bankrupt. BAS

WALNUT TREE
1 Walnut Tree Walk
c.1863 - current

c.1912

Long established Stowmarket builder Joseph Andrews completed this building in about 1850. Andrews lived next to the Red Lion in town and was employing 10 men by 1851. He owned the Walnut Tree until his death in 1893 at the age of 87. His executors looked after it until Greene King became the owners in 1898. A full licence was issued in 1953.

This pub has had many different addresses throughout it's history, one of these was 43 Violet Hill, and others were Childers & Part Childers. Like many other watering holes it started off life as part of a shop, the Stowmarket Courier of 1869 states that "Mr George Diaper was granted a new certificate in the room of Adelaide Ormes at Violet Hill". At one time the area contained several Walnut trees, & this is perhaps the reason the name was chosen. The earliest I can find The Walnut Tree name is 1881. BAS

Occupiers

1858-1864	George Ormes, a tailor/shopkeeper, died 1864 aged 33.
1864-1869	Mrs Adelaide Ormes, widow of George.
1869-1874	George Diaper & shopkeeper, age 27 in 1871, to Rose & Crown.
1875-1879	William Wright.
1879-1881	Nelson Andrews, a coach painter age 29 in 1881, he went to Hull.
1881-1882	Mrs Tabitha Bird, interim licence
1882-1896	Robert Mann & shopkeeper, coach builder's assistant only on 1891 census.
1896-1907	Mrs Susannah Mann, wife of Robert.
1907-1932	George Rope, protection order 1907, born c1866 an engineer.
1933-1938	Arthur Charles Dodson, went to Beyton Bear.
1938-1940	Harry Percival Pettit, from Bury St Edmunds.
1940-1943	Phyllis Pettit.
1943-1948	Cyril Godfrey John Mannall.
1949-1970	Jack Edward Ernest Holden & Olive, retired.
1970-1975	Eric R Christy & Nancy, quote from a local paper "born Witham Essex, 15 years in trade before Stowmarket, he will be a van salesman, lives in Lindsey Way in the town"
1975-1977	John & Susan Gardiner, from Hitchin Herts.
1978-1978	No name on electoral role.
1979-1992	Peter G Mayes.
1992-1993	Brian J Wood.
1993-	Lesley V Johnson
1994-1995	Derek Martyn.

1996-2000+   Derek P Smith, to Soham Cherry Tree.
2008-   Sue & Jerry Newman

WHITE ELM
Bury Road

A property named the White Elm is recorded back to at least 1692. It was situated on the Bury Road outside the town between Spikes Farm and The Tollgate. It was a farm, but also seems to have traded as a pub for a time. An advert in the Bury and Norwich Post of 1797 has "The White Elm Pub for sale" and John Roper as the owner.

A John Kent is at White Elm Farm in the overseer's accounts of 1814 and in 1816 he is reported to be changing his residence to his brewing office in Stowmarket and selling his farming stock. BAS

WHITE HART
[formerly Black Swan/Swan]
6/6a Crowe Street
1818 – 1967

This inn had been in existence for at least 135 years when Henry Ungless returned as innkeeper in 1818, he had been here some 14 years earlier before moving on to run other inns in the town. Henry may have been responsible for the name change. A previous inn with this name had existed in Ipswich Street until it's closure in 1808, it had been one of the premier inns of the town and the name may have been taken by Ungless to trade on the prestige of this earlier inn. Family history research into the Ungless family has also shown that Henry's grandparents may have ran an inn named the White Hart. The family had lived in the Laxfield area but the location of this particular White Hart is unknown, so there is also the possibility that Henry had renamed the inn in memory of his grandparent's inn. Whatever the reason the inn was trading under this name by July 1818.

Henry Ungless remained until about 1830 when he gave up The White Hart and became a commercial traveller for Messrs Stevens and Co. Brewers at their new brewery in Stowupland Street. He died of asthma in 1840 and his tombstone in Stowmarket churchyard described him as "many years innkeeper".

His tenure of the inn was not uneventful, as in 1824 a burglary was committed by a Joseph Carter and David Southgate who stole two saucepans, a boiler and a frying pan from Ungless, for this crime they received the death penalty which was commuted to the sentence of transportation for life.

Wm Walters in centre c.1901

In 1827 Ungless was accused of adding illicit compounds to his beer. In the case heard before Roger Pettiward and Edgar Rust, Justices of the Peace, he was accused of being in the possession of 1 pound of coriander seed and 8 ounces of vitriol, the implication being that he was adding these substances to his beer. By this time the brewing of beer for sale was tightly controlled by legislation and no other ingredients except malt and hops were permitted, certainly not vitriol! It was soon disclosed that Henry had received 2 parcels containing these substances via the London coach. Not knowing who had sent them he laid them aside on a shelf and forgot about them. The parcels had been sent by someone who had then informed the authorities resulting in a visit from the collector of excises and his clerk; Henry delivered up the parcels explaining how he had got them. He had to answer the charge, but his friends rallied round and his defence by William Ranson solicitor was paid for by "several respectable inhabitants of Stowmarket".

Apparently the person responsible for this scam was known and had tried something similar with a brewer at Rougham. Whether this was in hope of a reward for informing or from mischief is not known. After some discussion between the JPs the defendant was unanimously acquitted. At the hearing it was mentioned that beer was brewed at the inn and a man was employed for this.

In a sale of the inn in 1867 the property was described as *"very substantial buildings in good repair, good cellarage, entrance passage, commodious retail bar, bar parlour, market room, spirit store and counting room, upper floor a large clubroom, 4 chambers, also bottle washing house & sheds & stables with loft, having standing for upwards 20 horses, large yard with two carriage entrances."* It was sold for £750. Several of the larger inns had market rooms including The Fox and The Rose where farmers would meet to do business on a Thursday over a drink. From 1913 the Aggis Family were long associated with The White Hart, firstly Harry Aggis and then his son in law Sidney Crosby. Sid was closely associated with Stowmarket Football Club in the 1930s and The White Hart became the team's headquarters at that time.

In April 1967 after some 300 years use as an inn The White Hart closed. The building was taken over by R.C. Knights and Sons auctioneers; Knights ran the busy livestock market which was held to the rear of Crowe Street. Before this Knights had occupied the building adjacent which was now demolished to make way for Wilkes Way. NL

Owners
18?? – 1835	Mr. Aldrich
1836 – 1836	Messrs Marriott
1836 – 1837	Robert Paul
1837 – 1842	William Francis Paul
1843 – 1859	John H Cuthbert of Stonham Brewery Robert Smith and Spencer Freeman also shareholders at this time
1859 – 1865	Mr. Sedgwick of Stonham Brewery
1866 – 1867	Hansard J Bridges brewery
1867 – 1868	Bridges & Hunt

1868 – 1876	F. Hayward mortgagee
1876 – 1882	Michael Miles Cobb, 1880 meeting of his creditors
1883 – 1894	William Golland Ranson of Violet Hill Brewery, leased the inn
1895 – 1896	Phillip C.N. Peddar auctioneer
1897 -	Tollemache & Co.

Occupiers

1818 -	after 1830 Henry Ungless
1835 - 1836	Thomas Drew, sale of furniture Sept 1836
1836 - 1853	Robert Smith, a shareholder of the inn, age 47 in 1851
1853 - 1855	James Copeland
1855 - 1862	Edward Gibbs Cuthbert, tailor
1862 - 1865	George Davey, horsebreaker., robbed in 1865, bankrupt Jan 1866
1865 - 1866	Mr. Ryall
1866 - 1867	Hansard J. Bridges also owner
1867 - 1882	Michael Miles Cobb, mineral water maker, also owner, previously foreman at Gun Cotton Co
1883 - 1884	Jesse Keen
1885 - 1886	Alf Bullingham from Diss, 1886 fined for being drunk
1887 - 1889	David Stoneman, merchant of Lawford
1889 - 1892	Samuel Worrell, 57 in 1891
1893 - 1893	Thomas Tuthill, left possibly gone overseas
1893 - 1894	Mrs Anna Tuthill
1895 - 1898	Miles William Hubbard
1898 - 1903	Henry Thomas Arnold, pork butcher
1903 - 1909	William Walters
1909 - 1913	David Lenney
1913 - 1936	Harry Aggis
1836 - 1941	Sidney Mauldon Crosby from Dovercourt, married daughter of Harry Aggis
1941 - 1945	Harry Brown
1945 - 1949	Herbert Charles Goode
1949 - 1967	Jack and Ida Chenery, Ida also worked at Railway Tavern at one time

WHITE HART
Ipswich Street/Market Place
Before 1641 – 1808

Long after closure

In the Middle of the 17th century the town's principal inns were chiefly clustered around the Market Place. Possibly the largest inn in Stowmarket at that time was the White Hart Inn; this was situated in Ipswich Street facing the Market Place, and eventually became Turner & Co the grocers, latterly Woolworths and now Peacocks.

The first mention we have found of an inn of this name in the town is in 1645 when Robert Culham was landlord. Robert was in town by 1626, and in 1641 the churchwardens paid him for supplying dinners.

By December 1772 the coach Mercury was leaving the White Hart "to Finborough, Bildeston, Stoke By Nayland, Witham, Hatfield, and Chelmsford to Soho in London, every Tuesday, Thursday and Saturday at 5 o'clock, inside passengers at 18 shillings, outside ten and six, 14 pounds of luggage allowed". Samuel Elmer took over the inn in 1781 as announced in the Bury & Norwich Post, which added that it was lately in the occupation of his sister Mrs Ann Pooley. Samuel was still in occupation in 1798 when a Mr. John Elmer (his brother?) is at the inn and advertising in the Bury and Norwich Post for a "strong hobby, not more than 13 hands".

In 1800 Mr Rust the then owner was offering the inn to let. Robert Keeble took the tenancy; he had previously been at the White Hart in Colchester. Around this time the importance of the inn led to it being the venue for meetings both of local and county matters. In 1782 a meeting was held to raise a subscription for a 74-gun ship for the navy. The Bosmere & Claydon Association & a charity for the widows & orphans of Claydon used the venue. Another meeting was in the nature of a protest against new taxes at the time of the wars with France, and yet another protest was held against the tax on coal in 1793. But some meetings were of a patriotic nature, such as the one of Subscribers to the Defence of the Kingdom, which was addressed by Lord Euston, and another called to raise a "Company of Stow Hundred Volunteers" in 1798.

This use of the inn continued in the early 19th century, the Stow Hundred Association For Prosecuting Felons holding meetings there and also the Commissioners of the new Stowmarket Navigation. There were also auctions and entertainment, John Crosse an apprentice surgeon, in his diary mentions that he "went to a musical play at the White Hart" and "Played at a concert at the White Hart" in 1808. He also attended a Quaker Meeting at the inn in what he described as "The Great Room". It was this room, and the ability to accommodate a large number of people, together with Stowmarket's central position in the county that made the White Hart such a prominent venue. In 1808 a Mr. Boldero ended his tenancy with a sale of his effects, the inn was advertised to let and was put up for sale. In 1810 Mr. Joseph Lankester, grocer and draper moved into the building and the premises ceased to be used as an inn.

Lankester was one of a new wave of tradesmen who prospered from the Stowmarket Navigation, which had opened in 1793; other families included the Webbs at Combs tannery, the Fisons, and the Prentices. Manning Prentice had the premises next door for his grocery business and used the stables of the old White Hart. These families were Nonconformist and particularly of the Independent persuasion, they intermarried and the businesses they founded were to shape Stowmarket in the 19th and into the early 20th century. Joseph Lankester was able to use the extensive vaults of the old inn, which extended under Ipswich Street in his burgeoning Wines and Spirits business.

On the closure of the old White Hart, Samuel Waters saw his premises the Kings Head in Ipswich Street as successor to Stowmarket's premier inn, however the name White Hart was, after a few years used by Henry Ungless, anxious maybe to trade on the prestige of the name for his premises in Crowe Street which had previously been named The White Swan. NL

Owners
1658c - 1666	William Dow/Dove brewer
1684	Mr Barrill?
1714	Zachariah Seager
1714 - 1742	Charles Chesson, apothecary
1742 - 1779c	Margaret Chesson widow of Charles
1765 -	Thomas Rust, & Thomas Rout?
1806	John Edgar Rust, son of Thomas
1808	for sale, closed

Occupiers
1626c - 1655c	Robert Culham
1656c	William Cole
1666 - 1683	Edward Goodale
1683 - 1687	Thomas Offord
1688 - 1692	Thomas Martin
1692 - 1697	Isaac Page
1711 - 1712	John Pooley
1713 - 1748	Robert Hall father & son
1748 - 1768	Martha Hall widow, by 1750 the Post Office was housed in the inn
1768 - 1777	Joseph Lamb, from Greyhound
1777 - 1783	William Shave
1783 - 1787	John Pooley, from the Bell
1787 - 1791	Anne Pooley widow of John
1791 - 1799	Samuel Elmer, brother of Anne Pooley
1800 - 1804	Robert Keeble, from White Hart Colchester
1807 - 1808	Simon Boldero

WHITE HORSE INN
Stowupland Street/ 11 & 13 Station Road
c.1633 -1903

1902

A 15/16th century timber framed building given a brick frontage, the archway that led to the yard and maltings to the rear still retains a carved and moulded beam. This is also shown in a drawing by Edward Edwards of the early 1880s.

An early deed states that the house was "now known by the sign of the White Horse and previously known as Puckfenns". The White Horse traded as an inn for some 250 years.

When Richard Quash died in 1700 an inventory of his goods was taken listing the rooms at the White Horse as follows; cellar where there was beer and empty barrels stored, old beer buttery with more beer, cider and empty barrels, back kitchen, brew house, the yard with 2 pigs in a sty, hay chamber, hall, great parlour, middle parlour, little hall, and upstairs - kitchen chamber, parlour chamber, middle chamber, hall chamber and little hall chamber. Giving a house with 5 main rooms on each floor.

Even by the standards of the time which saw inn tenants change every few years this inn seems to have had a great many different occupiers throughout the 19th century.

A description in 1853 states that there was a large dining room, good parlours, porter rooms, bar, bar parlour, capital bedrooms, large brewhouse, store rooms, excellent cellars and stabling for 50 horses. A little later another sales description mentions 3 parlours, 5 bedrooms (as in the inventory of 1700) and stabling for 30 horses. In 1903 at a time when the number of licensed premises was being reduced this old inn was closed, probably because of it's proximity to the Queens Head. Today an opticians shop and a dental surgery occupy the building. NL

The White Horse Maltings 1883

Owners

1599-1634	John Barnewell esq of Stowmarket possible owner
1634-1637	James Barnewell of Dublin owner, brother of John
1637-	Richard Keyan (his will 1683, to wife Mary then son Richard) & Thomas Preston
1669-1700	Richard Quash senior
1700-	Ann Quash widow of Richard
17-- 1734	Jeremiah Bigsby
1734-1747	Jeremiah Bigsby junior
1748-1749	Chess Stedman, his wife Alice & Elizabeth Pearson
1749-1772	Samuel Rout
1772-1821	Thomas Rout part owner
1793-1806	George Holden part owner, third wife was widow of James Payne of Greyhound, George bankrupt 1805.
1815-1836	John Smith a butcher part owner (from Queens Head)
1818-1820	James Roberson part owner
1821-1821	James Ward, signed over his estate to John Stutter & John Garland of Bury St Edmunds brewers, & Peter Batterbee of Norton wine merchant.

18?? - 1829	Edgar Rout Buchanan part owner, bankrupt late Stowmarket sells his brewing utensils etc
1836-1853	Elizabeth Smith, & widow of John, her third share to be sold, stables 50 horses.
1853-1867	John Smiths exors
1867-	For sale, ground floor bar & bar room, 3 parlours, kitchen, tap room, first floor market room 5 bedrooms with attics, underground cellars, stables for 30 horses.
1868-1885	Charles Woods' Bacton Brewery
1886-1894	William Hammond
1895-1903	Greene King

Occupiers

1637 -1637	Robert Kemp
1669 -1700	Richard Quash owner/occupier
1711 -1715	Simon Wright
1732 -1732	Thomas Beast
1732 -1737	Edmund Mills
1737 -1742	Ann Halls widow
1745 -1746	Thomas Burch (from Flowerpot/Angel)
1746 -1750	John Garnham
1750 -1764+	Mr Rout owner/occupier
1773?-1781	Joseph Hines innholder/yarnmaker, buried 1782 Stowmarket age 27, from Bildeston
1794-1806	George Holden owner/occupier
1807-1815	Henry Ungless, & possibly with his brother William
1815 -1836	John Smith (from Queens Head) part owner/ occupier/butcher, buried age 51
1836-1841	Elizabeth Smith widow of John
1841-1843	Robert Thorns (from the Rose)
1843 -1846	Thomas Coleman junior
1847-1848	J W Robertson
1848-1853	William Last
1854-1854	O H Webb
1854-1854	J W & G Stevens (brewers)
1855-1855	Francis Stow, ex brewers drayman
1855-1864	William Mills, fined 5 shillings in 1860 for selling

	out of hours (ex wine merchants porter)
1864-1867	John Martin (a tailor from the Rose & then Railway Tavern)
1867-1869	Harry Gooding
1869 -1870	George Barker (retired innkeeper in 1861 age 73)
1870 - 1870	George Glasspoole, died age 75, from Admirals Head Little Bealings
1870 - 1871	Caroline Glasspoole, she married Wm Ruffell a blacksmith from the Barge
1871 - 1871	William Ruffell
1871 - 1873	Edward Baker, late of Finningham
1873 - 1877	William Green, to Duke of Wellington
1877 - 1880	William Freeman Woods from Bacton age 39, court case 1878
1880 -1880	George Everett from Ipswich interim licence
1880 - 1880	Thomas Proctor
1880 - 1880	Charles Abbott
1881- 1881	Robert George Parker & coal merchant
1881 - 1881	licence refused to Mr J F Fetham of Beccles
1882-1883	Thomas Samuel Woods
1883 -1885	Henry Victor Cornwall, to White Lion
1885 - 1894	James Cobbold, court case 1890, to Hop Pole Tavern
1894-1903	Frederick Bullock, had fowls stolen 1897, had glass broken 1897, buried 1903 age 37
1903 -1903	Sarah Ann Bullock

WHITE LION
Market Place
Mid 16th/early 17th century

The "old" White Lion stood in the Market Place occupying the shop that is now Holland and Barrett and the neighbouring property, also buildings in a yard to the rear confusingly known later as "the George Yard", the extent of the property is shown on an early 19th century plan found among parish charity papers.

The property was part of a charity which became known as the Old White Lion Estate, the rent being used to provide gowns for poor men and women with the letter M.F. upon them in remembrance of the donor Michael Flegg. Little is known of Flegg, a manorial document states that he had a house opposite the church in the Buttermarket. He is listed in Stowmarket in the 1568 subsidy returns, being apparently one of the the town's most wealthy residents, he died here in 1611. Unfortunately no will of his has been found, this would have detailed his bequest of the property. Both Hollingsworth in his History of Stowmarket and F.B. Marriott in his History of Stowmarket Charities mention the earliest then surviving deed of 1652.

There is no surviving record of this building's use as an inn, at the date of the endowment or soon after the property must have ceased to be used as an inn, as a "new" White Lion had been established in Stowupland Street by 1620.

From this evidence it is supposed that the "old" White Lion was trading sometime from the mid 16th to early 17th century. The property continued to be owned by the parish until the early 20th Century. NL

WHITE LION
Stowupland Street
c.1620 - 1892

The second inn of this name in Stowmarket. The earlier "Old" White Lion was in the Market Place, It has proved difficult to distinguish the two inns from each other during the early 17th century and there may be some confusion between the two but we have done our best to untangle the various references.

When it became an inn probably in the early 17th century this building was already ancient. A survey of 1991 on the surviving portion of this building ahead of the construction of Gipping Way, showed that it had been first erected in the late 14th century as a four bay artisan's dwelling, possibly including a shop with a typical medieval hall house layout. The northern three bays were demolished in the 1960s leaving just the southern bay.

After several phases of repair and modification the building became the White Lion, probably by 1617, the name recorded being owner Stephen Ward a feltmaker who died in 1647. Ward is mentioned in

1604 when his servant's name appears in the burial register. However, there is nothing to locate Ward at the White Lion that early. A list of money " layde owte aboute the repacon [repair] and charges of the Whighte Lyon" by Stephen Warde exists for 1622 in the churchwardens accounts. In 1638 some unknown travellers died while staying at his "house". Various wills and insurance policies show that the inn also had a brewhouse and stables.

At some date £40 from a charity, which had been bequeathed by Robert Aggas in his will of 24th April 1628, was invested in the White Lion Inn and premises, a rent-charge was regularly paid by the owner. The use the bequest was put to was a "good and Godly lecture and exercise of preaching of the Word of God, on the usual Market Day" for this "Two and Fifty Shillings by the year" was paid.

Despite being a little way from the centre of town the inn seems to have been a busy place, being often mentioned as the venue for auctions. Horses involved in local races were also stabled there on occasions as in 1772 when a race for a prize of £50 was run at Chilton Leys, the horses "Slipping Jack" and "Black Ey'd Betsey" being stabled at the inn. In 1749 the Ipswich Journal announced a "drawing match" at the White Lion. A drawing match was an event no doubt attended by wagers in which the relative strength of horses would be put to the test by them being required to pull wagons loaded with sand over a given distance, the difficulty was often increased by blocks of wood being placed in their path.

Among the hosts here were James Williams in the 1840s and 50s. James's brother Charles was at the Queens Head at around this time. Arnold Suttle previously of the Royal William was in residence here in the early 1870s before moving to the Dukes Head. In 1883 Edward Edwards sketched the view of the White Lion sign together with that of the Staff Of Life just over the other side of Stowupland Street.

After a succession of owners the White Lion was acquired by Alexander Clutterbuck, then owner of the Stowmarket Brewery eventually passing with the sale of the brewery to Edward Greene & Co. later Greene King. By this time the place had definitely come down in the world, being no more than a beer house which occupied a Victorian extension at the rear of the building.

A photograph from c1890 by Stowmarket photographer Arthur Bugg shows a crowd in front of the White Lion. A large water tank that may have been made by John Woods' factory in Bury Street is being hauled by horses. Stowmarket's police constable is closely watching the proceedings. Perhaps this was connected with the laying of water mains, this had commenced in 1887 by Messrs Greene King. The White Lion sign is visible behind, just the name by this time in place of the pictorial sign. Soon after, in 1892 the old White Lion closed its doors for good. By now there were another two beerhouses just over the road – the Staff of life and the Barge, these too would close in the next twenty years. NL

Owners
1617-1647	Stephen Ward
1???-1706	William Pettit junior
1706-17??	Robert Pettit
1725-1754	Nathaniel Fairclough
1754-1756	Elizabeth Fairclough, widow of Nathaniel senior
1756-1763	Nathaniel Fairclough junior
1765-1796	Robert Maltyward of Buxhall, died 1796 age 82
1796-1800	Mary Maltyward, widow of Robert, died 1800 age 82
18??-1835	Robert Aldrich
1836-1839	Harris Mills
1839-1876	John Miller, brewer & maltster of Walsham Le Willows
1876-1882	Alexander Clutterbuck, brewer
1882-1887	Edward Greene and Co. brewer
1887	Greene King

Occupiers
1678-1682	Thomas Offord, from Kings Arms, then to the White Hart
1683-1687	Henry Aldridge
1688-1702	Mary Skipper/Skepper
1706-1718	Margaret Shipp, widow of Thomas
1718-1736	Thomas Lockwood

1736-1751	William Tibbenham
1772-1774	Richard Pollard, notice of horse race
1784-1798	John Dennant
1799-1???	John Dennant & Co.
1813-1825	Thomas Balls, married Elizabeth Wells of the Fox & Hounds
1825-1827	Elizabeth Balls
1836-1839	Harris Mills
1839-1859	James Williams junior, previously at Porters Arms
1859-1866	Edward J Cole, carpenter, member of 6th Suffolk Rifle Volunteer Corps
1865-1867	George Death, charged with assault
1867-1867	William Death
1867-1877	Arnold Suttle, cattle dealer, involved in a bad accident in 1869.
1877-1880	Robert Brown, his horse died in a race in 1879
1880-1881	George Rouse, from Ipswich age 62
1881-1882	Robert George Parker, from White Horse
1882-1885	Frederic Donald Cobbe, carrier
1883-1884	George Taberner [part of property?]
1885-1891	Henry Cornwell, was at White Horse, a carrier age 33 in 1891 then moved to Exning
Closed	before April 1892

BREWERIES

THOMAS PRENTICE & CO
Stowupland Street

"This firm is something of an enigma, although small it was well known locally, but little is known of it's history" so writes C R Bristow in 1985. Here is what is known to the authors about Thomas Prentice the man & the brewing part of this company. Thomas was in town by 1820 with premises on Navigation Wharf; he was a maltster with interests in the corn & coal trades. From about 1837 until his death in 1852 he lived in one of the best parts of town at this time, namely Violet Hill. He was buried aged 58 in the Independent burial ground. However, some five years later with the impending erection of a new church on the site his family decided to have his remains moved to the (old) cemetery.

The company expanded into milling, they built an asphalt factory, an artificial manure plant etc & by about 1888 they had commenced brewing albeit on a small scale. It seems they supplied the private trade, mostly farmers, labourer's etc especially at harvest time. By 1896 the company is listed as brewers in Stowupland, Stowmarket, Ipswich & Copenhagen. There is an account in 1897 of brewery worker John Skase being charged with embezzling 8/8d from his employers. In 1917 the brewery suffered from a serious fire, the damage was estimated at £2,000, some £85,000 today. However they were still brewing in 1922 & were described as bottlers, brewers chemists & a chemical works, all this as well as being lessees of the Gas Works!

George Henry Barbrook a Stowmarket director of the company was granted a licence at the quarter sessions to sell beer & cider by retail, to be consumed off the premises. The brewery with it's four employees was sold to Greene King for £1,250 in 1934, (£63,600) their chief acquisition was head brewer F A Reddish. (Wilson 1983). BAS

STEVENS BREWERY
Stowupland Rd/17 Station Rd

Brother's John Wills & George Stevens founded this company in 1827; it seems they traded as the Stowmarket Ale Brewery. It was probably their father, another John who in 1811 was a wine & spirit agent for a London Company that helped them start up. At one time the brothers had offices in Union Street, they also owned three beerhouses locally, namely the Wellington Inn, the Retreat in Stowupland & the Royal William in Union Street. An advert' of 1856 states "the brewery is for sale by auction in London, & is producing upwards of 10,000 barrels per annum, the brewery has ample cooling, fermenting & tun rooms, ale porter & grain stores, malt & hop chambers, scalding room's etc". Also a dwelling house, workman's cottage & land, together with a 24 horse boiler etc. Seven public houses & twenty others held under leases for sale by mortgages. A similar advert' was run again in March 1857; this produced a sale to Phillips Brothers. BAS

PHILLIPS BROTHERS BREWERY

Brother's Francis, John & James Henry traded as the Stowmarket Brewery; this concern was the successors in 1857 to Stevens. John McLacklan was probably their brewer/manager. By 1864 the company had offices in Bury St Edmunds, & by 1868 at Ipswich. The breweries nine public houses were rented, those in Stowmarket were the Royal William, Bakers Arms, & in Stowupland they operated the Wellington & Retreat, in Combs it was the Gardeners Arms.

A store in Newmarket was also rented. On expiration of their lease in 1865 the premises in Stowupland Road were offered for sale "the Stowmarket Brewery, substantially built & comprising of 30 barrel copper, high pressure steam engine & a comfortable dwelling house, stable, two cottages, large yard etc". The highest offer was £5,050, (£371,000 today) it was withdrawn, put up again & knocked down to Mr Thomas for Messrs Phillips the previous tenants. They continued to brew until their bankruptcy in 1872. Adverts of 1874 announced the liquidation of Philips' Stowmarket Brewery, In June 1868 Francis Phillips "late of Stowmarket Brewery" had entered into a partnership with Frederick King to establish a brewery at Bury St Edmunds. BAS

ALEXANDER CLUTTERBUCK

Clutterbuck purchased the Stowmarket Brewery in 1874 for £6,650; the sale included stables, 14 horses, coach houses, cart-sheds, two cottages & building land. He also bought the unexpired leases of 24 pubs in different parts of the county for £750, plus the Royal William in Tostock with 5 cottages £775, Royal William Stowmarket £610, Stowupland Retreat & cottage £530. Clutterbuck came from Hertfordshire, in 1877 he supervised the opening of Lancaster Wells' bonded warehouse, in the same year he purchased the Violet Hill Nurseries (known as Bess Garnhams) for £3,500. Besides the brewery (manager George Taylor) he owned four beerhouses/public houses in town, i.e. Blue Posts, Norwich Arms, Royal William, & White Lion.

His brewery supplied the Stow Union with stout at one shilling per gallon & beer at 10d per gallon in 1880. He supplied free beer to the inmates at Christmas time. However things were not well & an advert' in 1882 the brewery together with a malt house, 35 inns, public & beerhouses, cottages, & land with the goodwill were withdrawn from sale in London after they failed to reach the undisclosed reserve. Later that year Clutterbuck sold out to Edward Greene for £26,000. Clutterbuck's wife Adelaide was the prime mover in the instigation of the Roman Catholic Church in town in 1879. She & her husband moved from Stowmarket in March 1882 soon after the death of their daughter Dorothy. An Ipswich Journal advert' of 1884 has " Mr Clutterbuck's furniture to be sold, has left the county". BAS

EDWARD GREENE & SON
Westgate Brewery Bury St Edmunds

Just a few notes on the Stowmarket side of this company. After the purchase of the brewery from Clutterbuck in June 1882 they employed managers to run the business, those known were Fred Greene in 1885/6, & Thomas D Smith in 1886/7. The company merged with the adjoining Bury firm of F. W. King in June 1887. BAS

GREENE KING BREWERY
Stowmarket

A few brief notes of this concern regarding the Stowmarket element. In March 1887 water mains & a reservoir were constructed holding 200,000 gallons obtained from an artesian well. Thomas D Smith, followed by Charles H Nice are two of the managers known in the early period. In 1893 the company had experimented with traction engines for beer delivery around town.

The waterworks were offered for sale to the council in 1906, but it wasn't until September 1920 that a resolution was finally passed to purchase it, the price was £9,500 (£273,500). The waterworks was demolished in 2000 except for the frontage on Station Road. The bottling store was closed in 1920; thereafter they used the Royal Oak as their offices etc. BAS

JACOB GREEN'S
VIOLET HILL BREWERY
19 Violet Hill Road Stowmarket

Jacob Green was the owner in 1850 of a malting/brewery in Violet Hill Road, it's possible he was born in Combs in 1798. The brewery had various addresses in a time before streets & roads were standardized, these were Part Childers, Childer Place, Childer Road in the lane, Violet Road & Finborough Road. The brewery owned a beerhouse located next door, this ran from circa 1850 to at least 1855, the landlord was William Abbott, he may have been born in Onehouse in c1794. After Jacob Green's demise his assigns ran the business until October 1865 when the brewery was sold to Hansord Jackson Bridges. BAS

HANSARD JACKSON BRIDGES'
VIOLET HILL BREWERY

Elmswell in 1819 saw the birth of a man that had a chequered career to say the least. He was baptized John Hansard, but seemed to have changed his name around sometime before his arrival in Stowmarket in about 1846. There he became a merchant, farmer and maltster. Whilst living in rented property with land at Lime Tree House Ipswich Road Stowmarket, Bridges also rented another property plus land in Bury Road, both of these houses were owned by Mrs Rout. He ran a corn & coal business in Stowupland Road until 1855. It is at this point that the local newspapers tell of another side to his character, in brief, Bridges, aged 35 years, whilst running his business in Stowmarket, was also the proprietor of the Vauxhall Brewery in Wandsworth.

He had "forged the acceptance of Mr Gill of Battersea, to the bill in question, which he had got discounted at the Ipswich branch of the National Provincial where he had an account which was overdrawn" the outcome of the trial was a sentence of four years servitude. Two months later Bridges was brought from Newgate prison for an examination for his bankruptcy. This was such an unusual case that the Secretary of State was involved, it seems there had never been one quite like this before. The prisoner had proven debts that exceeded £4,000 (£262,000 in 2009). The case was adjourned for five months. The outcome of the following hearing was that Bridges passed his examination for bankruptcy. Stowmarket in 1862 is the next time we catch up with him, he is a manager for the Stonham Brewery (later to be owned by Benjamin Dawson). He ran the Hop Pole Tavern for a few months, then went to the Horse & Groom in town for a couple of years. By 1865 he was still working for Benjamin Dawson & in the same year is listed as being at the Violet Hill Brewery, where he was also an agent for four different insurance companies. At this time the brewery was still owned by Jacob Green's assigns. Also in 1865 Bridges bought the Unicorn in Lime Tree Place & the White Hart in Crow Street. The last date we have of him in town is May 1867 when the assigns of Bridges' are selling his two Stowmarket pubs. Apparently he died in Belgium in 1891.

For more see Suffolk Chronicle 12/5/1855 & 21/7/1855 also 1/10/1855 & web site records of the Central Criminal Court at the Old Bailey. BAS

WILLIAM GOLLAND RANSON'S VIOLET HILL BREWERY

William was another of those Victorian gentlemen who seemed to be into many different occupations. Born in Triplow Cambridgeshire in 1835, he was by 1860 until about 1863 the Station Master at Stowmarket. The following year the directories inform us that he has a coal business at the Stowmarket & Needham Market stations, he was also an insurance agent. By July 1868 William was the owner of the Violet Hill Steam Brewery, and was still running his other businesses. He also owned pubs in Ipswich, Woolpit, Botesdale, Rickinghall, Debenham, Kenton and Naughton. The Bell Bury Road, the Prince of Wales Ipswich Street, the Vulcan Arms Bury Street were the town pubs he owned. The White Hart Crow Street was leased by him.

He fathered at least seven children; two of his sons namely Albert & George Arthur followed him in most of his enterprises. William decided to retire from the brewing business, he put the house (on it's one-acre plot) the brewery, along with it's 17 pubs up for sale at the Great White Horse in Ipswich in August 1896. The business was withdrawn from sale at £12,700, but the next month it was sold by private contract to the Honourable D A Tollemache for £12,000. Only the brewery was up for sale in February 1897, again it was withdrawn, this time at £715, and as before the premises were eventually sold a month later, this time to Edward Salmon for £640. Ranson continued with his coal business until at least 1901. The following entry is from the Stowmarket burial register "William G Ranson of 56 Constable Road Felixstowe, churchwarden for many years was buried February 7th 1924 aged 88 years". BAS

EDWARD SALMON'S VIOLET HILL BREWERY

As stated, Tollemache's Ipswich Brewery placed an advert for the sale of this property in February 1897. It adds that it had frontages on Violet Hill of about 65 feet, & Childer Road of 150 feet. The residence, malting, & range of buildings & garden had an area of just over one acre. Mr E Salmon bid £700 but the business was withdrawn from sale at £715. However, it was sold some 3 weeks later to Edward Salmon of Finborough Road for £640.

The sale also consisted of other beerhouses in Rickinghall & Botesdale. Edward was born in town in 1819 & was for many years an ironmonger, he retired to Finborough Road & it seems he purchased the brewery at about the same time. George Ranson, son of the former owner William, was in residence until at least October 1899. BAS

FRANCIS HERBERT CAVALIER'S VIOLET HILL BREWERY

I think the best way to record this story is to quote in the main from the Stowmarket Weekly Post of November 7th 1907. "At the bankruptcy court Mr Registrar Giffard heard an application for an order for the discharge from bankruptcy Mr Cavalier a brewer of 8 Cranbourne Court Albert Bridge Chelsea, lately carry on business at Violet Hill Brewery Stowmarket. The official receiver reported the bankrupt failed in may 1904 with provable debts of £1, 910 & assets which although valued at £2,031 had only realised £91/13/10. He returned to this country from abroad in 1895, & in the same year sold an estate in Ceylon of which he was the owner for £2,500. He was without occupation until February 1900, by which time his capital was reduced to about £750. In the same month he purchased some dismantled brewery at Violet Hill Stowmarket & a dwelling house adjoining for £750. He fitted up the brewery with plant & machinery

& made additions to the premises at a cost of about £1,700, all of which he borrowed & carried on the brewery until the end of March 1904 when in consequence of insufficient capital & falling business he closed it". Cavalier placed a manager in charge namely Christie Ahier Hipp from Hadleigh. Hipp applied for a licence to sell beer by retail, this was however refused, & he was still managing the brewery in 1904. Another snippet we found was that in May 1903 Robert Chilvers Cobb was charged with embezzling money from his master Mr Cavalier a brewer. To summarise the rest of the bankruptcy hearing, Cavalier attributed his failure to his inexperience in brewing, ill health, & bad management. He had tried unsuccessfully to sell the business in August 1903, but no bids were forthcoming. The official receiver opposed discharge on the grounds of insufficient assets, & imperfect book keeping, & his inability to pay 10 shillings in the £ to his creditors. An order was made to suspend the discharge for two years. BAS

VIOLET HILL BREWERY
(Suffolk Brewery)

The property was offered for sale in August 1904, it was purchased by Frederick Miller with Herbert Edward Miller as occupier & brewer. Frederick can be found on the 1901 census, he was a boarder in Chilton Road aged 36, he was a brewer's assistant, single, & born in Bethnal Green London. The business was a going concern in May 1910, but by September the following year it had ceased trading & a laundry was operating from the old brewery.

The owner was given as Millers executors, with a Miss Rayner running the business. In 1918 the laundry burnt down, it was however rebuilt & continued for many years. So after some 60 years & six owners the old brewery passed into Stowmarket's rich history. BAS

Catchpole beer label

Prentice beer lable C 1930

Oliver John Parker of Unicorn

Stowmarket Swifts Football Club :: ::

1923-24

President :—A. G. BRAMHALL, Esq.

Committee :—

H. Ager	E. Davey	R. Kemp
C. Bale	J. Francis	G. Melton
F. Buckle	C. Farrow	E. Pells
	W. Clements	A. Witton

Captain :—S. KING

Vice-Captain :—C. WYARD

Hon. Secretary and Treasurer :—
J. WEBB, Duke of Wellington, Stowmarket

Colours :—RED

Headquarters :—DUKE OF WELLINGTON

Ground :—CRICKET MEADOW

Duke of Wellington card first side 1923

THE SWIFTS FIXTURES 1923-24.

Date		Opponents	Com.	Ground	Result
Sept.	8	Coddenham	S	Away	
	15	East Bergholt	I	Away	
	22	Bramford Works	I	Away	
	29	St Peters and Grey Friars	I	Away	
Oct.	6	Claydon	S	Home	
	13	Brantham Reserves	I	Away	
	20	Bramford Works	I	Home	
	27	Finningham and Newton	I	Away	
Nov.	3	Needham Reserves	S	Home	
	10	Second. School Old Boys	I	Away	
	17	Needham	I	Home	
	24	81th Battery	I	Away	
Dec.	1	83rd Battery	I	Home	
	8	Finningham and Newton	I	Home	
	15	Stow Rovers	S	Away	
	22	Coddenham	S	Home	
	26	Debenham *Boxing Day*	S	Away	
	29	Hadleigh British Legion	I	Home	
Jan.	5	Elmswell	S	Away	
	12	Woolpit	S	Home	
	19	Needham	I	Away	
	26	East End Athletic	I	Home	
Feb.	2	Needham Reserves	S	Away	
	9	Brantham Reserves	I	Home	
	16	Claydon	S	Away	
	23	Woolpit	S	Away	
March	1	Stow Rovers	S	Home	
	8	St Peters and Grey Friars	I	Home	
	15	East Bergholt	I	Home	
	22	East End Athletic	I	Away	
	29	Hadleigh British Legion	I	Away	
April	5	84th Battery	I	Home	
	12	Second. School Old Boys	I	Home	
	18	Debenham *Good Friday*	S	Home	
	19	Elmswell	S	Home	
	26	83rd Battery	I	Away	

S—Stowmarket League. I—Ipswich League.

other side of Duke of Wellington card 1923